17830

E

BRISBANE

NEW
SOUTH
WALES

Barwon River
Macquarie River

BLUE MOUNTAINS

Lachlan River
Murrumbidgee River

River Murray (1st called Hume)

bendigo•
ntains   R Goulburn
•Maryborough   Mt. Disappointment   ALPS
•Ballarat   Gippsland
ELBOURNE
Geelong•
Bo   Port Phillip   Collins 1st settlement

Western Point
King Island   Wilsons Promontory   Flinders Island
Port Dalrymple   Georgetown   BASS STRAIT
                    Launceston

TASMANIA

rbour   Freycinet
                     Peninsula

HOBART

Port Arthur

Newc...
B...   Por...
Parramatta   SYD...
              Bota...

D1639361

JAMES COOK

Part of
AUSTRALIA

Peter Forster
1963

PEOPLE FROM THE PAST – No. 3
EDITED BY EGON LARSEN

IN A STRANGE LAND
Pioneers of Australia

William Charles Wentworth
From a portrait, painted c. 1860

IN A STRANGE LAND

Pioneers of Australia

THEO CARTER

LONDON · DENNIS DOBSON

First published in Great Britain in 1964
by Dobson Books Ltd.
80 Kensington Church Street, London, W.8

This book is copyright under the Berne Convention

© by Theo Carter 1964

PRINTED IN GREAT BRITAIN BY
C. TINLING AND COMPANY LIMITED
LIVERPOOL, LONDON AND PRESCOT

CONTENTS

A*

ILLUSTRATIONS

Author, editor, and publisher would like to express
their sincere thanks to the Australian News and
Information Bureau and the Librarians at Australia
House, London, for their great help in supplying the
illustrations for this book.

CHAPTER I

THE ELUSIVE
CONTINENT

WHEN Bartholomew Diaz first rounded the southern point of Africa during his voyage of 1486, he opened the sea route to the East, though more than three centuries would pass before men knew for certain all the lands which were to be found there. Eleven years later, his fellow-Portuguese Vasco da Gama voyaged as far as India. Columbus, seeking the East, had sailed west, arguing that if the world were indeed round, as some men said and as he firmly believed, he must in time arrive at the Indies. His reasoning was correct, but the islands he found were part of what was to be called America, though to his dying day he never knew it.

In 1520, Magellan coasted down South America and discovered the Straits that bear his name. He sailed into a new ocean which he named the Pacific, then turned northwest, later to die in the Philippines. One of his ships reached home in three years, making the first voyage round the world. For centuries brave and hardy seamen roamed the uncharted oceans, mapping new lands. Sir Francis Drake from Devon, in the *Golden Hind*, was the second captain to circumnavigate the globe, winning himself a knighthood from Queen Elizabeth I. Cartier, the

Breton, discovered Canada; Hudson and Frobisher sought vainly for a north-west passage that would enable navigators to avoid the icy south.

It was not only curiosity and love of adventure that drove the discoverers on. Many of them were little better than pirates, and the new lands held promise of treasure to be had for the picking. Spain quickly colonised the Caribbean countries and Peru. The British and French were active in North America. The Portuguese and Dutch were spreading over the rich spice islands of the East Indies. To reach these islands, the route was either northwest from South America, or north-east from South Africa. There was no reason for ships to venture out from this course into the vast seas which, as far as anyone knew, rolled emptily for thousands of miles across the Southern Hemisphere.

Yet this very emptiness worried the map-makers. It simply did not seem possible that all this water should have no land in it. Such a void was untidy, upsetting the balance of nature. In the fifteenth century, the astronomers had claimed, against great opposition, that the earth was not flat, but a sphere turning in space, and Magellan's circumnavigation had provided the final proof. It was hard to believe that water could adhere to a revolving ball with nothing to 'anchor it down' . . . though indeed if land *did* exist on the under side of the globe it must surely be uninhabited, for how could people themselves stay on it, walking upside down?

It was all very confusing, and a great deal of argument went on, but for a long time no one could be found willing to sail into the blue on an exploration so hazardous that they would be almost certain not to return. To make their minds easier, the map-makers arranged an imaginary coastline all along the bottom edge of their charts, labelling it 'Terra Australis Incognita'. This gave the maps a much better balance, and the haphazard outline did in fact roughly represent what is today the continent of Antarctica.

In 1567, an expedition from Peru, led by Alvaro de Mendaña, had discovered a group of islands east of New Guinea, which he called the Solomons, in the belief that they were rich in gold. Returning a second time, he could not find these islands again, but discovered the Marquesas. With him on this second voyage sailed Pedro Fernandez de Quiros, who came home convinced that a great continent did exist in the South Seas. For years de Quiros besought his king to furnish him with ships and men, and at last King Philip III of Spain sent him to the Governor of Peru, who provided three vessels for a new expedition.

Across the sunny Pacific they sailed. From one coral island after another, brown-skinned Polynesians with great mops of hair stared from dazzling white beaches, or put out in canoes from palm-fringed shores for a closer look at the strange vessels with the great square sails. At last, on a morning in the year 1606, land was sighted which stretched as far as they could see to the north and south.

De Quiros scarcely had time to christen his find *Terra Austrialia del Espiritu Santo*—Southern Land of the Holy Spirit—before his crew mutinied. At midnight on June 11th, his flagship *St Peter and St Paul* slipped out of the harbour, homeward bound for Peru, leaving the second captain, Luis de Torres, to command the remnant of the expedition. The crews of these ships, too, were restive, but Torres managed to calm their fears. After making sure that their landfall was not a continent but just another island (one of the group now called the New Hebrides), Torres sailed on to pass southward of New Guinea, being the first European captain to sail through the straits between that island and Australia which long after were given his name. He actually sighted Cape York on the mainland, but thought it must be one more island. Thus Torres missed the honour of discovering Australia, and went home to assert that there could not possibly be a continent in that part of the world.

De Quiros and Torres were Spaniards, but at that time the Dutch also were displaying interest in the great southern continent. From their colonies in the Spice Islands—they had established themselves in Java in 1598 —they were in a good position to investigate. They published beautiful maps of the islands, piecing together the outlines of the northern and western coasts that lay contiguous to the East Indies.

From Java, in March, 1606, they sent out a small ship, the *Duyfhen*, or Dove, which sailed into the Gulf of Carpentaria and half-way down its eastern side. The Dutch sailors who landed were the first Europeans to set foot on Australian soil, but so many were killed by the natives that the captain quickly went back on board and sailed for home; he called the place of their disaster Cape Keer-weer or Turnagain. The captain imagined that the coast of New Guinea was joined to the mainland, so the Dutch map-makers were misled; and the existence of the continent still remained a dream.

But now something happened to bring discovery

nearer. Ever since the Dutch had colonised the Spice Islands, their sea-route had been that first followed by the Portuguese, via the Cape of Good Hope to Madagascar, then in a north-west slant across the Indian Ocean to Java. It was a disagreeable and toilsome voyage. To lie becalmed in the tropics for weeks was a normal experience, like that of the Ancient Mariner whose ship 'lay idle as a painted ship upon a painted ocean'. But in 1611 a commander named Hendrick Brouwer tried out a new idea. After leaving the Cape, he sailed due east for three thousand miles before steering north to the tropics. On this course he had the advantage of favourable winds that blew him along far quicker than any ship that had travelled east before. He informed the Dutch East India Company, and in consequence instructions were issued that all their ships should follow this route.

It is evident that any ship on this new course would be far more likely to sight the western coasts of the 'great southern continent', and this is just what happened. On October 25th, 1616, the Dutch vessel *Eendracht* ran off course to eastward at a latitude of 26° south, and the captain, Dirk Hartog, landed on an island which now bears his name. On a post he nailed a seaman's pewter plate, hammered flat, recording the details of his visit. Dirk Hartog's plate, now one of the most precious treasures of the Rijksmuseum in Amsterdam, is the earliest memorial of European contact with Australia.

Now a real landmark existed. The Land of the Eendracht (T'Landt van de Eendracht) appears on several early Dutch maps, though they still showed the coastline linked with New Guinea. Locating other landfalls was only a matter of time. The whole land-mass was named

13

New Holland; the south-west corner, discovered in 1623, was Leeuwin, meaning the Lioness, and in 1626 the captain of a ship named the *Gulden Seepaart* sighted part of the coast fringing the Great Australian Bight, and called it Nuytsland, after a high official who was travelling aboard his vessel.

So now the world knew that east of longitude 115° there was land; whether it consisted of many islands or was all in one piece was still open to question. In August, 1642, the Governor of the Dutch possessions in the East Indies, Anthony van Diemen, sent his friend Abel Janszoon Tasman out with two ships to make discoveries in the South Seas, with the Instruction: 'All continents and islands which you shall discover, touch and set foot on, you will take possession of on behalf of Their High Mightinesses the States General of the United Provinces.'

Sailing from Batavia in Java, Tasman circled the Indian Ocean, then ran south. Meeting bad weather, he moved back into warmer seas, sailing rapidly before fair winds along latitude 42°, till on November 24th the cry went up 'Land ahead!'

The look-out had sighted the rocky shores of the island he charted as Van Diemen's Land, which later was altered, in memory of its discoverer, to Tasmania.

Tasman planted the flag of Prince Frederick Henry, Stadtholder of the Netherlands. After a couple of weeks, he was again heading east, and after nine days sighted the southern island of New Zealand, which he believed to be part of the great southern continent. Three of his crew were killed by Maoris in Massacre Bay during their landing in what Tasman recorded 'appears to be a very fine country'. He returned to Batavia via the Friendly Islands and the north coast of New Guinea, after a ten-month voyage of extraordinary significance.

But important as it was to know that these lands existed, none of the discoverers had so far done more than go ashore for enough time to plant a flag or look for water. The first man who took the trouble to try and learn something of the interior and its inhabitants was the Englishman, William Dampier, and he was not favourably impressed. As a young man, Dampier had gone to Jamaica to manage an estate but, not taking kindly to slave-driving, he joined a band of the Spanish Main buccaneers who made the lonely coves their headquarters. From then on, he lived a life of lawless daring—'Yo-ho-ho and a barrel of rum'—becoming one of a company of pirates who voyaged round the world, plundering on their way.

After several months of roistering in the China Seas, they put in to a place now known as Buccaneers' Archipelago on the north coast of Australia, remaining there for several weeks. These were the first Europeans to hold any communication with the Australian natives. Dampier had a flair for writing a picturesque narrative, and the published account of his travels caused a sensation.

Now rich, he retired from piracy to go back to England and buy an estate. His book, *A New Voyage Round the World* (1697), made him famous, but respectability was too dull. He requested the government to give him a ship to return to the great unexplored land, and in 1699 in the *Roebuck* he was back, sailing from Shark Bay on the west coast nine hundred miles to the north-west, of which he published a full account—full but depressing. For the inhabitants he had not a good word. 'They are the miserablest people in the world. The Hodmadods of Monomatapa, though a nasty people, yet for Wealth are Gentlemen to these, who have no houses or skin Garments nor fruits of the earth . . . setting aside their human shape, they differ but little from Brutes.' On his last voyage, which he made as a pilot, he met and rescued Alexander Selkirk, later immortalised as Robinson Crusoe by Defoe.

The discoverers of Australia

At least, said Dampier, he had the satisfaction of having discovered the most barren spot on earth. It was unfortunate that his descriptions of the parts he visited turned the tide of discovery away from New Holland for many years to come. For nearly a century, no one thought further of sending ships to find out more of such a miserable country.

However, an important discovery was indirectly brought about in 1770. Scientists of The Royal Society in

London had calculated that the planet Venus would cross the disc of the sun in 1769, and that this could be observed in particularly favourable circumstances in the South Seas. The Society requested the Admiralty to furnish a ship, equipped with instruments to observe this phenomenon, and a 370-ton ship, *Endeavour*, was refitted for that special service. The scientists aboard included a wealthy botanist, Joseph Banks, and the whole expedition was placed under the command of James Cook, a naval lieutenant of the highest character, thereafter to become world-famous as Captain Cook. A Yorkshire boy, he had been a shop-assistant at thirteen, thence went to sea as apprentice in a coal vessel, contriving in the intervals of a rough life to educate himself in navigation, astronomy, and mathematics. Entering the Royal Navy, he soon rose in rank, and in his work of surveying the coasts of North America he was already on the way to becoming one of the great cartographers in history.

The transit of Venus having been duly observed at Tahiti, Cook opened a sealed envelope containing his further instructions, and read: '. . . whereas there is reason to believe that a continent or land of great extent may be found . . . you are to proceed southward in order to make discovery of the land abovementioned, or fall in with the land discovered by Tasman now called New Zealand.' There followed long and detailed directions to observe tides, currents and soundings, soil, beasts and fowls, and the genius, temper, disposition and number of the natives; ending with the command: 'You are also with the consent of the natives to take possession of convenient situations in the country in the name of the King of Great Britain. 30th July, 1768.'

So Cook ran south to look for the elusive continent. Not finding any land, he made for New Zealand, where he found that this consisted of two large islands separated by what was to be called Cook Strait. He stayed there for six months, charting the coast so thoroughly that later a French navigator wrote: 'I found his chart of an exactitude and thoroughness which astonished me beyond all power of expression.'

Now Cook turned his attention to the Terra Australis Incognita. Was it the country the Dutch had called New Holland, of which the west and north was already partly known? Its eastern boundaries had never yet been visited. He resolved to sail westward from New Zealand 'until we should fall in with the east coast of New Holland, and then to follow the direction of that coast to the northward, or whatever other direction it might take us, until we arrive at its northern extremity'.

On April 18th, 1770, Cook's Journal records: 'Last night we saw a Pintado Bird and several Albetrosses . . . the first of these birds are certain signs of the nearness of land . . .' And on April 19th: 'Saw land.' Northward sailed the *Endeavour*, and on April 29th dropped anchor in a large bay. Next day they went ashore. Several natives were on the beach, and Cook seemed surprised at not being able to understand a word they said. The first meeting was rather unfortunate, for when the English 'threw them some nails, beeds etc.', the natives made some gestures that caused the landing party to 'fire two Musquets, which we had no sooner done than they throwed two darts at us'.

Cook's opinion of the natives, however, was a great deal better than that of Dampier: 'They are of a middle stature, straight bodies and slender limbed, their skins the colour of wood or dark chocolate, hair mostly black. Their features are far from disagreeable and their voices are soft and tunable. They may appear to some to be the most wretched people on earth, but in reality they are far more happier than we Europeans; being wholly unacquainted not only with the superfluous but the necessary Conveniences so much sought after in Europe, they are happy in not knowing the use of them. They live in a tranquility which is not disturbed by the Inequality of Condition; the Earth and the Sea of their own accord furnishes them with all things necessary for life; they covet not Magnificent Houses, Household-stuff etc., they live in a warm and fine climate and enjoy a very wholesome Air, so they have very little need of Clothing, and this they seem to be fully sensible of, for many to whom we gave Cloth left it carelessly on the Sea beach and in the woods as a thing they had no manner of use for. In short they seemed to set no value on anything we gave them, nor would they ever part with anything of their own for any one article we could offer them. This in my opinion argues that they think themselves provided with all the necessaries of life and that they have no superfluities.'

So wrote Captain Cook, unaware that the coming of the white man signalled the beginning of the end of the happy tranquility of the aborigines.

During the stay in harbour, Cook had the British flag displayed on shore every day, and an inscription was cut in a tree setting forth the ship's name and the date. The name of this historic spot almost became Sting Ray Harbour, owing to the immense numbers of these fish seen. However, wrote Cook: 'The great quantity of New Plants etc. Mr. Banks and Dr. Sollander collected in this place occasioned my giving it the name of Botany Bay.'

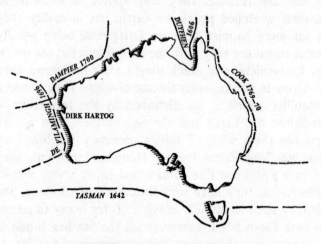

Voyages of discovery around Australia

CHAPTER II

'A COLONY OF
DISGRACEFULS'

Two weeks before Christmas, 1773, a whooping party of
American colonists disguised as Mohawk Indians stormed
aboard a British ship in Boston Harbour and threw overboard a number of chests of tea. The famous 'Boston
Tea-Party' was the best known of many protests against
the tactless administration by the Government of King
George III of its American colonies, a discontent which,
a year and a half later, resulted in the War that led to
the formation of the United States.

The American War of Independence violently affected
the whole history of the world. One immediate result,
which at the time seemed more of a minor nuisance than
a far-reaching effect, was that English gaols became
crammed far beyond their capacity, and even the 'hulks'
—disused ships moored in the rivers, where convicts
rotted for years—were nearly bursting at the seams. No
longer could gaolbirds be shipped off to Virginia to be
sold for a few pounds to work in the tobacco or cotton
fields, as had been the convenient and profitable custom
for more than sixty years, and the state of the prisons
soon became a public scandal.

In eighteenth-century England, the noble and land-own-ing families were the unquestioned rulers of society. Occasionally, a poor relation or the son of some worthy servant might aspire to moderate advancement through some such personage; but anyone without a patron, however gifted or hard-working he might be, would be lucky indeed to rise above the station into which he had been born.

For those at the top, life was extremely agreeable. Servants ministered to every need. Property was sacred, and the laws against stealing were savage. The man who poached a fish to feed his starving family, the boy who picked a pocket or the servant girl who stole a spoon risked transportation for seven years. This was the penalty for; among other things:

Petty larceny, or thefts under one shilling.

Stealing fish from a pond; fishing in enclosed ponds or buying stolen fish.

Stealing roots, trees or plants of the value of five shillings.

Stealing a shroud out of a grave.

Watermen carrying too many passengers on the Thames, if any drowned.

Sheep stealing was punishable by death. But life was so hard that many people took the risk of large crimes as well as small, for, as they said, 'you may as well be hung for a sheep as a lamb!'

Not that the ruling classes were consciously cruel. All they desired was a comfortable life, with everything unpleasant swept out of sight under the rug. Even before the loss of the American colonies, there had been talk of finding some new place for the ever-growing numbers of prisoners. Joseph Banks, soon to become Sir Joseph, had

22

suggested Botany Bay to a Committee of the House of Commons in 1779 as a possible Receptacle for Convicts, but nothing had come of it at the time. However, the war had thrown up another problem, that of the American colonists who had sided with the British, and for whom defeat meant ruin. A new place had to be found for these 'loyalists', and one of them, James Matra, who had also sailed with Cook in the *Endeavour*, approached Lord Sydney, then Secretary of State for the Home Department, suggesting that New Holland might be the answer. Discussions dragged on till suddenly matters were brought to a head.

In the gaols and hulks—where simple folk whose only 'crime' was some such misdemeanour as poaching a fish or a hare, were cooped up together with hardened criminals—the dirt, vice and fevers of various sorts had risen to a point that the City Sheriffs became seriously alarmed. In a deputation to the Government they warned in strong words that unless the hulks were cleared, and quickly, the terrors of the Great Plague might soon descend again upon London.

This bombshell had immediate effect. The 'loyalist settlers' were left to work out their own problem, and soon we have Lord Sydney writing to the Lords Commissioners of the Treasury:

My Lords,

The several gaols and places for the confinement of felons in this kingdom being in so crowded a state that the greatest danger is apprehended . . . I am commanded to signify to Your Lordships His Majesty's pleasure for effectually disposing of convicts and rendering their transportation reciprocally beneficial both to themselves and the State by the establishment of a colony in New South Wales, a country which, by the fertility and salubrity of its climate connected with the remoteness of its situation (from whence it seems hardly possible for persons to return without permission) seems peculiarly adapted.

Location agreed upon, a suitable commander had to be selected for the convoy transporting convicts to what some wit described as 'the Colony of Disgracefuls'. Obviously there was no point in wasting a man who might be useful at home; could not some retired naval officer, competent but undistinguished, be found?

The choice fell upon Captain Arthur Phillip, aged fifty, son of an English woman and a German teacher of languages, as first Governor and Captain-General of the new colony. After the French War of 1778, he had retired to Hampshire to try his hand at farming. Perhaps his German blood accounted for his methodical thoroughness and 'unflappability'. His sense of duty was absolute. More by lucky chance than due to anyone's foresight, he proved to be the perfect man for the job. Unemotional and completely honest, he had the maddening characteristic of being always right.

He was right about one thing which everyone else at that time would have regarded as utterly absurd. Phillip thought of his Colony of Disgracefuls as potentially an important part of the British Empire. The collection of criminals and trouble-makers whom the Government could not get rid of quickly enough were as unpromising material as could be found; but that vision was the only thing that enabled Arthur Phillip to surmount the almost unbelievable difficulties that faced him in the days ahead.

The convoy, known to history as the First Fleet, assembled at Spithead in March, 1787, remaining there until May. The Commodore's flagship, H.M.S. *Sirius*, was an old victualling ship of 540 tons, picked up cheap and made into a man-o'-war by the addition of a few ancient cannon. With the brig *Supply*, a storeship of 170 tons, the fleet consisted of six transports carrying 759 convicts and three food ships. Phillip fought for decent tools, for overseers and skilled men to build the new settlement, but the Government was grudging and everything supplied was of the most wretched kind.

Bulkheads filled with nails ran between decks, with loopholes to fire muskets down in case of trouble. The decks were crowded with pens containing sheep, hogs, goats, chickens, turkeys, geese, ducks, pigeons, and cats, and more stock for breeding was to be taken on at the Cape of Good Hope. The marine officers, prepared for a long stay, brought furniture and household goods—including a piano. The convicts, bound for an even longer term, were not so well provided for. They had almost no clothes or possessions of any kind; even their official documents were left behind so that there was no way of checking their names, crimes, and lengths of sentence.

The fleet set sail on May 13th on a course via Teneriffe, Rio de Janeiro, and the Cape of Good Hope, arriving in Table Bay on October 13th. They had had fair weather most of the way and owing to the Commodore's careful supervision of food and conditions, their health was generally good. Shortly after leaving South Africa, Phillip decided to shift his pennant from the *Sirius* to the *Supply*, which was a better sailer. He took with him the three fastest transports, but he beat the rest of the fleet by only one day—Captain Hunter was a very fine navigator.

Mr. Joseph Banks had described to the House of Commons Committee 'miles of fertile meadows, long and luxuriant grass and a good supply of water' to be found at Botany Bay. The new arrivals, however, saw a place with no water, no shelter, surrounded by bogs and swamps. So, leaving the ships at anchor, the Commodore and Captain Hunter went exploring northward, through a gap in the cliffs which Cook had charted as Port Jackson.

No sooner were they through the heads of land than their shouts of joy showed they had found a harbour 'where all the navies of the countries of the earth could anchor in safety . . . the finest harbour in the world'. They did not know then that it was surrounded by the most miserable country on earth.

Having explored the harbour, and selected—and named—Sydney Cove as the place of anchorage, Phillip returned to Botany Bay and ordered the fleet to make ready to move, himself going back to the cove with a picked crew to prepare for the landing. While he was absent, an unexpected incident took place.

The last of the fleet had scarcely come to anchor on January 23rd when two ships suddenly appeared in the offing. They did not enter, but quietly disappeared into the mist. Who could they be? the men asked each other. English, with more convicts? Dutch, to oppose a landing? Captain Phillip thought they were French ships, of which several were engaged on voyages of discovery in the South Seas. He gave orders that no person should go on board if the ships came into harbour; and no sooner was he out of sight than the ships appeared again, entered the harbour, and cast anchor.

This put Captain Hunter in a dilemma. He sent off a boat extending a courteous greeting 'as from host to guest'—there was to be no doubt about that. The convoy turned out to be French ships under the command of the Marquis de la Pérouse, engaged on scientific discovery and with no designs to colonise the land. Cordial relations were established, and before the French ships departed the English officers were entertained several times on board. The Sydney suburb overlooking 'Frenchman's Bay', the meeting place, is to this day called La Pérouse.

A tricky wind was blowing as the English fleet hoisted sail, causing much difficulty in tacking round the coast into Port Jackson. Lieutenant Clark wrote in his journal:

> The *Prince of Wales* and we got a fowl of each other; what damage we did her I cannot say as I did not like it; if it had not been by the greatest good luck we should have been both on the rocks . . . and we should have gone to pieces in less than half of an hour, but how good the Almighty is to us.

However, all reached Sydney Cove without further incident. As they dropped anchor in the deep water off the cove, most of those on board eagerly scanned the wooded slopes for fruit and green vegetables and game for the pot—any relief from the everlasting salt meat and ship's biscuit.

The Governor and the marines and convicts who had come in the *Supply* had not been idle. A party had erected a flagstaff, and at sunset a ceremony was held. The flag —not the Union Jack, which did not come into use till after the Union with Ireland in 1800—was displayed, when the marines fired several volleys, between which the Governor and the officers drank the health of His Majesty and the Royal Family, and success to the new colony.

The date was Saturday, January 26th, 1788, a date which is still celebrated as a public holiday—Australia Day.

Disembarkation continued over many days. First the animals were slung off and put to graze. For the first few weeks the convicts were sent ashore to work by day, and back to their ships at night.

The work of clearing trees and building shelters called for able-bodied labourers; but the sullen and apathetic prisoners showed a marked reluctance to work, and who was there to force them? Despite Captain Phillip's entreaties, no overseers had been sent with the Fleet. Major Ross, Commandant of Marines, was adamant in his refusal to allow his men to play the rôle of prison warders. The Governor's only recourse was to appoint 'trusties' from the less ill-behaved convicts, and gradually some sort of work force was got under way. Axes swung to clear the trees. One party set up a blacksmith's forge, others were dragging loads of stones. Officers pitched their tents. Fires blazed up to cook the provisions, the same old salt pork they hoped soon to exchange for the fresh meat and fruit which this South Sea island would surely provide.

Almost before the landing was completed, a new embarkation took place. A thousand miles due east, Cook had charted a tiny green spot in the Pacific as Norfolk Island. For all that anyone could tell, New South Wales itself was just another small island exposed to attack from marauding French or even pirates, for whom Nor-

Botany Bay, 1770:
Captain Cook hoists the British flag
From a painting by T. A. Gilfillan

Australian Aborigine

Captain Cook

folk Island would be a perfect springboard; so Phillip's orders were to colonise it with all speed.

Off sailed the little *Supply*, a Noah's Ark carrying a few selected convicts and '6 ewes, 2 boars, 3 sows, a goat, 4 hens, 1 cock, 3 ducks and a drake', to start another colony from scratch under Lieutenant Philip Gidley King, R.N. The thirteen square miles of fertile Norfolk Island were a better proposition than Sydney Cove, and in fact more than once they served as larder in the cliff-hanging days to come.

Like so many other things in this strange land, the behaviour of the natives—whom the men called Indians —did not run true to form. All experience in colonising 'black' countries showed that the native inhabitants, after a more or less violent resistance, were brought to heel and became servants to the white invaders. But the New South Wales natives did not resist. Their first reaction to the fleet had been excited surprise. Clearly the fair-skinned men, in their ships like great birds, were supernatural beings. Captain Phillip's personal approach, unarmed and smiling with gifts of beads and looking glasses, met a friendly but guarded response. Curious, standing apart, they watched the happenings of the first few days. The man-animals, some of them shambling in iron chains, puzzled them; their friendliness was tinged with horror as some of these creatures were flogged, and with disgust when an executed wretch was left hanging on the newly erected gallows as a warning to all.

In every prisoner's mind there was but one thought— escape. In the first days many made off into the trees, but those who survived soon crawled back exhausted, mad with hunger and thirst. Their efforts were futile against

B

this land that resisted them at every turn. The escaping convicts did enormous harm in turning the natives against the invaders of their homeland. Taking out their injuries on savages whom they regarded as even more degraded than themselves, they threatened the aborigines and stole their spears and fish-hooks. To a community holding all property in common, theft was shocking. However, the 'Indians' reasoned that this must be a white man's custom, and any removable objects that took their fancy, from spades to hens, began to vanish from the settlement's meagre stock.

Spades were something that at first they did not understand. As the colonists discovered, the aborigines did not till the land. They grew no crops but lived on snakes, lizards, grubs, roots and such fish as they could catch, with an occasional kangaroo or wallaby killed by their spears. The soil round Sydney was so poor that it seemed as though nothing would grow in it. To make matters worse, almost no one among the settlers knew anything about farming; the convicts, allergic to work of any kind, deliberately destroyed many of their tools.

They had landed in the scorching southern midsummer. February came in with thunderstorms. Five sheep were struck by lightning; newly-begun huts were washed away over the flooded ground. The settlers had their first intimation that the climate of their new country, whether in flood or drought, came in out-size. When the last of the transports sailed away, they were marooned indeed.

The first little stunted crops came up—to feed the rats and mice. Native dogs called dingoes ate five more of the sheep. Six of the precious cattle wandered off into the bush. Everyone thought the natives had stolen them, but these two bulls and four cows lived on to become part of history. The lack of fresh food in this unnatural country was a bitter disappointment. No wild fruit grew in the bush, only a herb they called 'sweet tea' which could be infused into a drink. Now and then a kangaroo or wallaby was brought down, but apart from that or an occasional fish, the settlers were still living on the salt meat they had brought with them, now three years old and full of maggots. Almost everyone began to suffer from scurvy.

After much thought Governor Phillip ordered Captain Hunter to proceed in the *Sirius* to the Cape of Good Hope to buy grain. The two experienced officers decided that to avoid battling against the prevailing westerly wind it would be better to sail East and risk the dreaded passage round Cape Horn.

Hunter sailed at the end of September, leaving the settlers to work and survive as best they could. One of the busiest men was the Reverend Richard Johnson, who almost daily performed some marriage ceremonies, nearly as many burials, and a surprising number of christenings among the 'broad-arrow babies'—as they were called after the Government brand on the convict uniform. To everyone's surprise, they grew strong and flourished in the kind of life into which they had so fortuitously been born.

Mr. Johnson was a worthy man, but glum and completely lacking in any sense of humour. On the first Sunday after the landing on the barren shore, he preached under a large tree to his fettered flock from the text: 'What shall I render unto the Lord for all his benefits toward me?'

Following his instructions—and his natural instincts as

31

well—Governor Phillip was making attempts to establish good relations with the aborigines. In the early days these 'Indians' were shy but friendly and extremely curious, hanging round the settlement to watch the strange behaviour of the white men. They were happy, laughing people, fickle and lazy, who had no taste for any exertion except that necessary to secure their meagre food.

Governor Phillip

As sign language was not getting anybody very far, the Governor decided to try and capture a couple of them so that in time each colour would learn something of the other's language and customs.

Soon, two apprehensive 'Indians' were living at Government House. One, Colbee, escaped, but the other, a strong and amiable young man named Bennelong, earned himself a modest place in history.

He took a strong liking for English ways, and—too much considering the shortages—for English food. Quickly picking up the language, he grew devoted to Governor Phillip, who took him to England, where the 'wild man' caused a great sensation; he was even presented to King George. Sent home after two years, he was rejected both by his own people and by the whites, took to drink, and died miserably. But it is on Bennelong Point, where he had his house, that Sydney's Opera House stands today.

Bennelong proved a valuable go-between on exploration parties into the bush. The rather starchy Governor Phillip seemed able to relax with the blackfellows (as those who began to learn English called themselves) in a way he never could with his own men. Journals kept by the settlers are full of stories of encounters with the stone-age ladies, who proved to have a lot in common with more modern members of their sex. Wrote Dr. White, Surgeon-General to the First Fleet and prolific journal-keeper, in his diary: 'My companion continued to exhibit a number of coquettish airs while I was decorating her head, neck and arms with my pocket and neck handkerchiefs. The buttons of my coat I tied round her waist with string. Ornamented and delighted, she turned from me with a look of inexpressible archness.'

Travelling northward by boat, they found that Broken Bay formed the outlet of a great river, which they named the Hawkesbury, with miles of flat land along the banks which might well prove fertile, but the attempted return overland turned out to be much too difficult. Hungry men have little energy for exploration, and famine was approaching with giant strides. Their shoes were worn out, the once smart uniform coats were ragged and torn. Not only their cloth, but their nerves also were wearing thin.

In this unnatural life, tempers became frayed to breaking point. Savage floggings were meted out to convicts and even to marines for trivial 'crimes'. Many starving men were hanged for stealing food—in one case even for stealing some soap, value 8d.

Major Ross, commandant of the Marines, had not needed privation to sour his temper. From the first, he had been a thorn in Phillip's flesh with his constant bickering. At one time, he had more than half his officers under arrest. Two of the surgeons rushed out into the night after a disagreement to settle matters with pistols, before, as another chronicler, Lieutenant Clarke, recorded, 'the Governor convinced the two sons of Esculipious that it was much better to draw blood with the point of their lance from the arm of their patients, than to doe it with pistol balls from each other.'

Captain Hunter brought the *Sirius* back within seven months—then a record for a voyage round the world. During that time the rations issued to the settlers became smaller and smaller, till the supreme thought in the minds of the little band clinging to the desert shore was: 'When will food come? How long can we hold out?' The flour brought by *Sirius* staved off hunger for a few months; then anxiety began again. It seemed that as far as England was concerned, the Colony of Disgracefuls had been abandoned: 'Out of sight, out of mind, and jolly good riddance!'

The Governor took a desperate decision. He would send the *Sirius* to Norfolk Island, then on to China to buy provisions. Lieutenant King should sail in her, and from China he was to make his own way to England with despatches describing the desperate straits the colony was in. Perhaps Lord Sydney had fallen from power, and his successor had forgotten all about New South Wales?

When the *Sirius* sailed on March 27th, the weekly ration was down to 4 lb. of flour, 2 lb. of salt pork and $1\frac{1}{2}$ lb. of rice per head. This was not the sudden belt-tightening of healthy men; they had been half-starved for more than a year, with bodies crying out for everything we know as vitamins. Livestock broke into the gardens to steal the miserable crops. Men were too weak to work; the weather was wet; the huts fell down; and several of the men went mad.

Could they hold out, or would the ships return to a place of the dead?

On April 5th, the signal went up: 'Sail sighted'. Captain Tench of the marines wrote in his journal: 'We were surprised to see a boat known to belong to the *Sirius* rowing towards us. Plainly something disastrous had happened. A few moments turned doubt into certainty; to our unspeakable consternation we learned that the *Sirius* had been wrecked at Norfolk Island on the 19th of March.'

For the first time Governor Phillip felt that to make an absolutely personal decision was too much responsibility. He called a 'Council of War'. It was decided to send the *Supply* to the East Indies with instructions to hire another ship from the Dutch and load her as well.

But even with the greatest speed, she could not make the double journey in much less than six months—and starvation was much nearer than that.

Again the ration was cut. No one thought of anything but food. All boats were commandeered for communal fishing, marksmen were sent out to shoot anything they could see. A man caught stealing potatoes was sentenced to receive three hundred lashes—if the flogger had the strength to lay them on; and to be chained for six months to two similar thieves—if all of them lived that long.

Gradually all work ground to a standstill. Only the Governor retained the will to inspire hope. By the end of June, even on starvation rations, they would have eaten the last of their salt pork. Then, on the evening of June 3rd, came the joyful cry: 'The flag's up!'

But the *Supply* could not be back yet. Frightful memories of the wreck of the *Sirius* fought in all minds with the hope of a new ship from England; yet a new ship it was indeed, the *Lady Juliana*. Those who rushed out to meet her in small boats could read her name as she lurched up the harbour after almost foundering on the rocks outside.

How much food had she aboard? Little enough. She brought 222 female convicts and the shattering news that the Second Fleet was close behind with nearly 1500 convicts and three ships' companies, all needing to be fed! Another piece of news was that a store ship, the *Guardian*, loaded down with supplies for the colony, had been wrecked off South Africa in the preceding January. If this vessel had arrived, all the starvation and suffering would never have happened. After all, they had not been abandoned by the old country!

THE WONDERFUL
KANGUROO,
FROM
BOTANY BAY,
(The only One ever brought alive to Europe)
Removed from the HAY-MARKET, and now exhibited at the LYCEUM, in the STRAND, from 8 o'Clock in the Morning, till 8 in the Evening.

THIS amazing, beautiful, and tame Animal, is about five Feet in Height, of a Fawn Colour, and diftinguifhes itfelf in Shape, Make, and true Symmetry of Parts, *different from all other* QUADRUPEDS. Its Swiftnefs, when purfued, is fuperior to the Greyhound: to enumerate its extraordinary Qualities would far exceed the common Limits of a Public Notice. Let it fuffice to obferve, that the Public in general are pleafed, and beftow their Plaudits; the Ingenious are delighted; the Virtuofo, and Connoiffeur, are taught to admire! impreffing the Beholder with Wonder and Afto-nifhment, at the Sight of this unparalleled Animal from the Southern Hemifphere, that almoft furpaffes Belief; therefore Ocular Demonftration will exceed all that Words can defcribe, or Pencil delineate........Admittance, ONE SHILLING each.

From a London handbill in the early nineteenth century. The picture was first published as an engraving in Captain Phillip's *Voyage to Botany Bay* (1789)

CHAPTER III

THE SECOND FLEET

THE joy caused by the arrival of the *Lady Juliana* died down when, in a few days, three more transports were seen struggling up the harbour.

The Second Fleet was the worst blot on the whole history of convict transportation, and those present when the holds were opened to discharge the human cargo were never likely to forget the scenes they witnessed on that harrowing day.

The frightful conditions may be blamed on the system whereby the Government contracted for shipping the convicts at the rate of so much per man. The more prisoners carried, the higher the fee, and a proportion of deaths on the voyage was accepted as a matter of course; but never had anything been seen like the arrival of the *Neptune*, the *Scarborough*, and the *Surprise*, of which the first was the most terrible of all. Seventeen hundred convicts had been embarked, two hundred corpses had been thrown overboard during the voyage, and on arrival hundreds more were in the last stages of illness and exhaustion. Many died when brought up into the sun and air. Few had the strength to enter the boats, and for the most part the wretched creatures were slung over the side in nets, like animals. For weeks afterwards, bodies were washed up on the beaches round the harbour.

Even in case-hardened Sydney indignation was roused, and the reports that went back to England raised a scandal which forced an investigation into the disgrace of the convict ships.

Among the new arrivals were two men whose coming affected the whole future of New South Wales: John Macarthur, who was to dominate the colony for the next thirty years; and a young Irish ex-medical student named D'Arcy Wentworth, who was almost immediately posted to Norfolk Island as Assistant Surgeon. Among the convict women sent to the island there was a girl named Catherine Crowley, sentenced for a trivial misdemeanour, who had also travelled in the hell-ship *Neptune,* and a few months later her and Wentworth's son was born—William Charles Wentworth, who in his turn was to become the colony's most powerful personality.

With the arrival of the Second Fleet a change came over the settlement. Within a few weeks, two well-loaded store-ships arrived, lifting the threat of famine. Furthermore, the Fleet had brought relief for the Marine garrison in the persons of 350 officers and men of the New South Wales Corps, a regiment specially recruited for service in the colony—and the wife and young child of Lieutenant John Macarthur, Elizabeth and her son Edward.

The Macarthurs had taken passage in the *Neptune,* but even before leaving England the Lieutenant had been so appalled by the quarters offered that he had fought a duel with the captain; his disgust reached such a point that he insisted on having himself and his family transferred to the *Scarborough* in mid-ocean. At the Cape, Macarthur was laid low by a grave illness, of which one after-effect was a ruined digestion. Henceforth he would need to watch his diet, and hard liquor was poison to his delicate stomach. In the rough-living, deep-drinking community for which he was bound, a compulsory vegetarian and teetotaller would need a hard shell to protect him from his fellows. In John Macarthur's case, self-esteem was protection enough. His defence lay always in attack. Young as he was, this shrewd and arrogant man was soon to become the most important personality in New South Wales.

The wattle-and-daub house where Mrs. Macarthur took up residence quickly became the centre of the colony's society. With the exception of Mrs. Johnson, whom she described as 'the clergyman's wife in whose society I could find neither profit nor pleasure', the charming and cultivated Elizabeth Macarthur was the first English lady to set foot in New South Wales.

The house-with-piano—of Surgeon Worgan, temporarily posted to Norfolk Island, was soon the headquarters of the 'intellectual set' headed by Captain Tench of the Marines, debonair Man of the World, who later published two 'best-sellers' about the colony; and there was scientifically-minded Lieutenant Dawes, builder of the observatory. These people were joined by everyone else who longed to drink a cup of tea in an English drawing-room again, and to attend parties, picnics and excursions upriver to Parramatta, where the land was beginning to show signs of cultivation. Even the rigid Governor Phillip unbent to Elizabeth, and at a time when everyone bidden to dine at Government House had to bring his own bread, a note on his formal invitation read, 'There is always a roll for Mrs. Macarthur'.

A new trend had begun. So far, the settlement had been run on the basis of a kind of paternal socialism, with the Governor as supreme head. But by now many convicts had served their terms; officially they were free men, but there was no way for them to leave the country: they had no money to buy passages home, and the captains of the few ships calling were unlikely to take them on as crew; and very strict watch was kept for stowaways. So they began to work for themselves, to take up land grants and open shops; some, like Simeon Lord, to lay the foundations of great fortunes, to become respected citizens and magistrates. These ex-convicts, known as 'emancipists', looked down on the newly arrived felons; in their turn, they were looked down upon by all those, rich or poor, who had come out to New South Wales of their own free will. Several distinct classes were emerging: Exclusives (comprising officers and rich free settlers); poor free settlers; emancipists; and convicts under sentence, who possessed no rights whatever.

The divisions which from now on would harrow colonial society were beginning to show.

On St. Valentine's Day, 1792, Major Francis Grose, Commandant of the New South Wales Corps, stepped ashore from the transport *Pitt*, and his coming changed the whole balance of the colony.

A genial veteran of the American War, he was still troubled by his old wounds. By nature indolent, he cast his eye round for some ambitious, intelligent young officer to do the donkey work for him so that he could enjoy a life which promised to be considerably more pleasant than he had been led to expect. 'I like it here,' he declared, and was well content to hand over the chores to young Lieutenant Macarthur, now restored to health and obviously just the dynamic deputy his commanding officer wanted. 'An old head on young shoulders,' said the Major of him.

So John Macarthur became Regimental Paymaster, business organiser, and behind-the-scenes power man of the colony. Already in his first dispute with the Governor, Macarthur won. It concerned the landing of a keg of spirits, intended for the regimental store. Palmer, the Government Commissary, tried to seize it; Macarthur protested, His Excellency exploded, the Lieutenant talked back and was wrongfully threatened with arrest. Next day, the cask arrived in the store. The Governor had climbed down, but during his last months in the colony all invitations to Government House were haughtily refused by Mr. Macarthur.

For Arthur Phillip was going home. Over the years, a pain in his side had worsened until treatment in England was imperative. During his last year there had been many clashes. Phillip disapproved of officers on duty setting themselves up as farmers with assigned convict servants. The New South Wales Corps officers had arrived with just that purpose in their heads, and a tired and sick man could not stand up to the new wave.

Arthur Phillip had given the colony self-respect and confidence in a just, impartial government, but the man who is always right is seldom loved. His unpopularity hurt him, and, being lonely, he threw himself with unswerving persistence into the shaping of his forlorn colony into what he hoped would one day become a nation.

On December 11th, 1792, Governor Phillip sailed out of Sydney Heads.

A holiday feeling was abroad in the settlement. The strict schoolmaster had gone, Christmas was coming, Goodwill to All! Cheerfully the officers clinked glasses, sardonically the convicts clanked their chains. For John Macarthur, spending the festival in the bosom of his family, his drink was water, his Christmas dinner a plate of vegetables. Dyspepsia was troubling him, but materially his prospects looked pretty bright.

Major Grose, the new broom, had great plans for reorganisation. For his right-hand man a new post was created—Inspector of Public Works—and Lieutenant Macarthur, at the age of twenty-six years, became to all intents and purposes manager of the developing colony. How many servants might be assigned to an officer? Which men should be selected? What permits should be granted? Apply to the Inspector for everything; apply almost for permission to breathe. Unpopular he might be with some, but the Corps stood solidly behind him.

As far as development wss concerned, the two and a half years when Macarthur was virtual master were the most productive of the first twenty years. Every soldier who wanted them got his twenty-five acres, every freed convict thirty. The only trouble was that there was not enough convict labour to go round, and in any case the convicts had a rooted dislike for work. Chains and the lash could not force them. Money? The colony had no currency, and there was nothing to buy that would lighten their dreary lives.

Nothing? Yes, there was one thing that could bring a laugh and help them forget their fate: *Drink. Spirits.*

For a can of grog they would risk the cat-o'-nine tails; they would even bestir themselves to hard work. Drunkenness in those days was nothing shameful, it was looked upon as a matter of course in all classes, and an unlimited quantity of raw spirits was always coming in as news spread in foreign ports of the insatiable thirst of Sydney Town.

It is hard for us to understand how life can be carried on with no official coinage in circulation, but that is how it was for the first twenty-five years in New South Wales. When the penal settlement was instituted, everything—rations, building materials, clothing—was issued from Government stores. Naval and military personnel were paid with credit bills on the British Treasury, for there was nothing in the colony to buy, and primitive barter was the only form of exchange. When the first farms began to produce grain, payment for it was made by a receipt from the Commissary; these receipts passed as coin and were accepted by masters of incoming ships; when they accumulated they were returned to the Commissary, who gave a bill on the Treasury in London.

Of course there was graft. Some Commissaries issued their own private notes which passed from hand to hand with inflated values. Everyone who was smart got into the act—Sydney harboured many expert forgers. From visiting ships trickled in coins from Spain, Holland, China and India to create a black market in foreign exchange, run by smooth operators. In 1799, the British Government shipped out £1,100 worth of pennies, halfpennies and farthings! Pocket-money weighed more than a ball-and-chain, but not till 1813, at the prolonged entreaty of

Governor Macquarie, did £10,000 worth of Spanish dollars arrive to form the colony's first legal currency.

For the officers of the New South Wales Corps, imbued with the notion of purchasing goods from incoming ships and selling them at a profit, neither farthings nor ducats were going to make their fortune. But ships' captains would accept their credit notes on the Treasury in London. So they could buy up cargoes and resell them on their own terms; by operating as a 'ring', they could make a profit of up to 500 per cent on the commodity that was more precious than gold or diamonds . . . rum.

So rum became the currency, used in exchange as money. Everyone was in it—there was no other way to buy or sell. Business was booming, and Grose's command, known as the Rum Corps, rose on the crest of the wave.

Though no new Governor had yet arrived, Major Grose sailed for England on December 17th, 1794, leaving in nominal charge Captain Paterson, a modest naturalist whose only desire was to be let alone and not be bothered —a wish fully in accordance with the policies of the Inspector of Public Works.

The obsession with rum had reached the point when workers would accept no other payment. Materially the results were imposing. The colony's economic structure had been transformed by the new set-up. For the first time, New South Wales was feeding itself—when it wasn't drinking itself to death.

In the years between 1793 and 1796, Great Britain was conducting a series of rather unsuccessful military operations against the French revolutionary forces. France had conquered the Netherlands; she controlled the Dutch fleet and virtually the Spanish fleet as well. Deserted by her allies Russia, Prussia, and Austria, Britain was left to 'go it alone' against Napoleon, the young military commander whose star was rapidly ascending.

It was not surprising that the authorities in London, having all this on their minds, were somewhat remiss in despatching a successor to Governor Phillip of the penal colony of New South Wales. To Britain, this speck in the South Seas, which had been a tiny experiment in the great business of administering an Empire, was turning into an expensive nuisance.

Though Phillip recommended Lieutenant P. G. King, who had made a good job of colonising Norfolk Island from scratch, the post—after three years' delay—was given to Captain John Hunter, late commander of H.M.S. *Sirius*. Hunter was a protégé of Admiral Lord Howe, and it occurred to no one that the qualifications possessed by a fine seaman and navigator might not be those needed to cope with the tricky problems which New South Wales had already begun to pose.

Hunter was a Lowland Scot, an honest old salt with the reputation of being unlucky. When he arrived in H.M.S. *Reliance* in September, 1795, he naturally turned to his former friends in the colony and to his naval colleagues of the voyage out. It took him only a few weeks to give mortal offence to the officers of the Rum Corps.

Almost before he had settled in, a man brought a piece of news, relayed from the Indians, of a great herd of wild cattle grazing in pasture land finer than any yet seen, about fifty miles away up the Nepean River. His new Excellency well remembered the black day soon after the first landing when the precious two bulls and four cows had vanished into the bush. Could these much-lamented animals have escaped aboriginal spears and discovered the pastures sought in vain by the settlers? Thrilled and excited, the Governor decided to go and see for himself.

He invited David Collins, the Judge-Advocate, to accompany him. Commanding the *Reliance*, which had brought him out, was Henry Waterhouse, veteran midshipman of the First Fleet; he had to come too, and so had the ship's young surgeon, George Bass. But where were the unofficial rulers of New South Wales? Where was John Macarthur, in whose career these cow pastures were to play so large a part? None of them was asked to the picnic, and this omission was the first step in the Governor's downfall.

For forty years, John Hunter had served his country afloat, working his way up the ladder from captain's servant to be captain himself. Accustomed to naval discipline, where a hoarse bellow from the quarterdeck pulverised any tendency to independent thought on the part of underlings, he had no idea how to cope with the spirited young officers who for nearly three years had been lording it over the colony. As the months rolled on, jealousies and bickerings flared up from nothing. Magnificently reliable at sea, Captain Hunter was a natural muddler at an administrator's desk.

One of Sydney's oldest Inns

CHAPTER IV

MEET MASTER WENTWORTH

THE small boy stood in the blazing sun, watching the red-coated soldiers as they marched from their barracks to mount guard at Government House. The dust they raised tickled his nose. Dust lay everywhere in Sydney Town—on the little dwellings of mud-and-wattle and in their scorched gardens, on the log gaol and the brick public buildings, on the white, ant-ridden house of Governor Hunter. The beauty of the natural scene—sparkling blue water against the trees that grew right down to the shore —contrasted sharply with the squalor of the white men's efforts to scratch a foothold in an ancient land that resented their intrusion.

The scar called Sydney, gashed in the trees edging the circular cove, had never been intended as more than a temporary base. Better country would soon be found. But the men of the First Fleet had discovered that the land extended not welcoming arms, but a clenched fist; the thick, arid vegetation that covered it, the *bush* as the aggravated English soon began to call it, stood guard to prevent any advance. In eight years the colonists had sailed up the harbour and built a few houses at the place called Parramatta by the natives, but the seat of govern-

49

ment was still Sydney, with its buildings projecting at all angles into roads that ran crazily to avoid tree-stumps—there had never been time to grub them out. Below the water tanks, the stream, once so sparkling, was murky with cast-off rubbish, sewage, and the washing of ragged clothes.

The boy slid over the fence, scuffling his feet in the dust. Behind the lumber-yard, the first swish of a cat-o'-nine tails brought forth a scream of agony that sank to jerked animal noises as the flogger laid on the sentence of fifty—or perhaps two hundred—lashes. Little William Wentworth avoided the road leading to the flogging post; such a sight was too ordinary to be interesting. That convicts must be flogged was something he had never questioned. They were creatures lower than men . . . lower than animals really, for animals were valuable and had to be cherished. If a convict died, that was one mouth less to feed, and there was a never-ending supply from England to fill their places. The boy was in a hurry now to catch Lieutenant Flinders when that exciting young sailor came off duty.

The first months after H.M.S. *Reliance* had brought William and his family from the green spot in the Pacific to the mainland had been rather lonely ones, as the boy's two brothers were rather young for company. On Norfolk Island, where his father had been not only Assistant Surgeon but also Superintendent of Convicts, William and Lieutenant-Governor King's son Phillip (with two 'll's', after the first Governor), who had been born a year after himself, were little Lords of the Earth. Convict servants ran to do their bidding. Whenever a ship came in, officers and sailors alike made much of the boys and held them rapt with tales of life afloat.

No adventure stories came up to those of Matthew Flinders. To the two small boys, the young midshipman of the *Reliance* seemed a being from another world, as indeed he was. Hero worshipping, they sat enthralled as he told how, at sixteen, he had set out on a voyage round the world under the famous Lieutenant Bligh, who was making a second attempt to transplant breadfruit from the South Sea islands to the West Indies. Bligh was a story in himself. On his previous voyage he had been cast adrift in the Pacific by a mutinous crew, but he was such a good navigator that he brought the boat safely across nearly four thousand miles of ocean.

'Papa says Bully Bligh is a foul-mouthed old sea-monster,' piped up little Phillip. But Flinders laughed, saying that Mr. Bligh may have been tyrannical and overbearing, but that he himself had no complaint against him.

'When I grow up I'll be a sailor too, and find islands of my own,' declared the future Admiral King, more prophetically than he could know.

As a relief from the squabbling military, Governor Hunter turned with delight to the activities being carried out along the coast by Midshipman Flinders and his friend, Surgeon George Bass. Both hailed from Lincolnshire, and were possessed by a madness for exploration. Hunter, who had himself spent thirteen years mapping the coasts of Canada and Newfoundland, encouraged them in every way. Stowed away in the long boat of the *Reliance* had come their eight-foot boat, *Tom Thumb* as they called her—and within a week of their arrival in Port Jackson they were off through the Heads sailing round to Botany

Bay. Caught in a storm, they feared for their lives. When at last they got through the breakers, everything aboard, including their gunpowder, was soaked. Busily absorbed in spreading the powder on the rocks to dry, they were startled to see a group of natives watching them intently.

'Weren't you afraid they might be cannibals?' asked the enthralled young Will Wentworth.

'Very much afraid indeed,' Flinders admitted, 'if they were, we should not have lived long enough to see ourselves boiling in their pot. Luckily I remembered how the Indians love having their hair cut. Dr. George had his surgeon's scissors, and by signs we suggested becoming their barbers.'

'Did they understand?'

'In time they did, looking as scared as we felt ourselves. But once I began to cut, broad smiles spread across their faces. I was almost tempted to see what effect a little snip might produce, but our situation was too critical to admit of such experiments.'

After several dangerous and exciting days they had got back in time for Flinders to rejoin his ship for the voyage to Norfolk Island. Bass occupied that time on an expedition to the Blue Mountains, that jagged range which caged the settlers into a strip of some thirty-five miles, and whose ascent had been attempted by many climbers from Governor Phillip onwards. Now Bass, equipped with rope ladders and grappling irons, made his attack on the confused and barren ridges riven by unscaleable chasms, but like all the others he had to admit defeat. Not for another seventeen years would three men conquer these rugged mountains, and one of them would be the boy who listened entranced to the story of fifteen days of unparalleled danger and exertion related by George Bass.

But it was not by mountaineering that Bass wrote his name on the map. Mariners sailing north from Van Diemen's Land had long suspected from the fierceness of the tides that a great river or strait existed in the neighbourhood of latitude 40°. Bass discussed this with Hunter, who said: 'Go and find out. I'll give you half a dozen seamen and provisions for six weeks.'

So George Bass, who was, after all, a surgeon and not a trained sailor, went off into the unknown in an open whale-boat, discovering and mapping natural harbours, till he rounded the south-eastern tip of New Holland to find that the strait existed indeed. Beating eastward against terrible weather, he entered a huge harbour which he named Westernport, where the party remained exploring for thirteen days. Nearly three months passed before they returned to Sydney Heads, having explored six hundred miles of coast and proved Van Diemen's Land to be separated from the mainland by the strait to which his name was justly given, Bass Strait.

Tall, handsome George Bass standing up in little *Tom Thumb* had been called the candle in a candlestick. He was a hero now. The following year Hunter gave Flinders the sloop *Norfolk*—his first command—and the two sailed through the strait and round Van Diemen's Land, discovering not only the beautiful Tamar River, but also that far-from-beautiful yet endearing Australian animal, the wombat.

A few weeks more and they were back on board the *Reliance*, sailing off round Cape Horn to South Africa to buy food for the larders of New South Wales—a memorable voyage, for the purchases made by Captain Waterhouse and Captain Kent of the *Supply* were to lay the foundations of Australia's primary industry: wool.

In the fast-developing weaving trade of Europe, no sheep was as highly esteemed as the merino, with its high-bridged nose and the great folds of fleece that could be spun into the finest wool. The breed was peculiar to Spain, whose government forbade export of rams or ewes on pain of torture or death. However, from time to time a few of the precious sheep were smuggled out—some to the Royal flock at Kew belonging to King George III, and some to the Dutch Government at the Cape. By chance a few of these came on the market just at the time when those two English sea captains went on a shopping trip to buy stock on their own account for resale in New South Wales.

After passing his examination for Lieutenant at Cape Town, Flinders had been appointed to the *Supply* under the command of his friend, 'Whiplash' Kent, Governor Hunter's nephew and a seaman from the age of twelve, who could hold any leaking hulk together and make her sail. In his journal Flinders wrote how, the ship being overloaded with Government stock, Captain Waterhouse gave up his cabin to the cattle he had bought, while Kent's own was full of merino sheep looking down their noses at such cramped accommodation. Across the grey southern ocean they sailed back to Port Jackson. Of the merinos that survived, some were sold to the Reverend Samuel Marsden, a better farmer than parson; four ewes and two rams went to John Macarthur at the price of thirteen guineas each.

At Elizabeth Farm, his flourishing estate in Parramatta,

Macarthur had been experimenting for some time with the breeding of sheep, crossing Irish ewes with rams from Bengal. The fleeces of these new beauties far transcended anything he had yet seen.

'They must be kept absolutely pure—no more cross breeding here,' he declared. His wife watched him pacing the veranda, his shrewd dark eyes half closed in concentration. His face was a mirror of his character, with its blunt pugnacious nose, its defiantly protruding lip. In his uniform of scarlet and yellow, with his white-powdered hair and queue, he was a striking figure. 'How bountifully Providence has provided for us,' his wife had written in a letter to England. 'I can truly say no two people on earth are happier than we are.' It was hard for her to understand why Macarthur was in such constant strife outside his home, where men called him arrogant and overbearing, a firebrand and a trouble-maker. Look at the miracles he had wrought here at Elizabeth Farm, the showplace of the colony, with its hundred acres of grain and vegetables and fruit trees, all achieved in a few years from virgin soil! If only people would take his advice, thought Mrs. Macarthur, all this feuding and fighting would cease and the affairs of the colony could be conducted in an orderly manner.

His wife's thoughts exactly matched Macarthur's own. He considered himself peculiarly under the protection of Fortune, which after all was only what he deserved. So deeply did he feel this that even the slightest disagreement with his opinions would freeze his expression to one of outraged haughtiness, while active opposition aroused his implacable hostility. Never had he been known to hesitate in a course of action that might make an enemy. In a hot climate where transactions frequently took place between men more or less fuddled with rum, Macarthur the non-drinker held what some called an unfair advantage. A cold man, the violence of his temper ran below a surface of icy self-control.

Like every civil and military officer, he was engaged in the rum traffic, for the barter of spirits had become the colony's way of life. Governor Hunter, instructed to put down the private selling of liquor, was helpless against the whole well-organised system. Every outgoing ship carried despatches from His Excellency complaining bitterly of the disorganisation, vice and general chaos of the colony which he was supposed to control. On nearly every page the name of John Macarthur appeared as that of a defier of authority and arch-instigator of everything that was going wrong.

More intelligent and far-seeing than most of his companions, Macarthur had soon realised that if the colony were ever to become anything better than a prison, it must be self-supporting. The results of his experiments with the new sheep convinced him that the obvious export commodity would be fine wool from fleeces such as he and the Rev. Samuel Marsden were beginning to produce.

In this he proved right. Like Arthur Phillip, he was usually right; but unlike the former Governor, his zeal for the public good always turned out to be at the same time for the benefit of John Macarthur himself: that the two paths so often ran side by side was purely coincidental. Now, sick of the constant bickering between all the would-be rulers, he took a big risk and committed what amounted to an unforgivable sin against Authority.

Over the Governor's head he wrote to the Duke of Portland, Colonial Secretary in London, reporting clearly on conditions in the settlement and concisely setting out his suggestions on the way in which it ought to be run. He well knew the sensitive spot in the Government's attitude to New South Wales—that it was costing too much and returning nothing. He offered a solution. In his opinion, from which he never wavered, the country's development should lie not in small agricultural farms, but in large properties run by an *élite* of graziers with capital and experience. He wrote, that his experiments in the cross-breeding of sheep had convinced him that by the raising of fine wool New South Wales could not only become self-supporting, but at the same time supply an urgent need of the mother country.

The Duke of Portland, himself a great landowner, read this report with approval. For months he had been receiving violent and contradictory despatches from Governor Hunter, excusing, appealing and protesting about the settlement which Major Grose, by his own account, had left in such an excellent order. Indeed, the latest letter begging for a supply of slop clothing 'because the colony is entirely naked' bore out Macarthur's insistence on the need for a local wool industry. Obviously this young soldier was a man of integrity, risking his own future in an attempt to stop the rot. The next despatch from Hunter, peppered with complaints about the gallant captain, drew a resounding snub.

Lacking any experience in diplomacy, the testy old Governor was floundering towards official suicide. With a six-month lag between England and the colony, quite apart from frequent shipwrecks, a question argued by mail could take several years to resolve. But for once the British Government was taking action. Long ago, Governor Phillip had recommended Captain P. G. King as his successor. Now, in November, 1799, thanks partly to the influence of Sir Joseph Banks, King was at last to return to the colony—as successor to Governor Hunter.

Philip Gidley King was no longer the sprightly Lieutenant who had done such a good job of colonising Norfolk Island. In 1795, he had been so ill that he was given up and later went back to England for medical treatment. Sickness and financial worry over the support of his family had turned him into a bald, gout-ridden man who looked far older than his age. His new appointment had not been obtained without constant badgering of the authorities in Whitehall; long delays in getting a ship had dug deep into his meagre resources, and when at last he sailed, he was £400 in debt. Almost throughout the voyage, fear of capture by the French fleet vied in his wife's mind with anxiety about his health: 'King very ill, gout flying about him' says her diary of the *Speedy's* voyage, which King himself called 'pleasant and expeditious'.

On arrival in Sydney, King's first duty was a most unpleasant one. Governor Hunter had no idea that his reign was over, and his successor had the difficult task of delivering the despatches telling him that he was deposed.

It was a bitter blow, and Hunter, licking his wounds, prolonged the embarrassing interval before his departure to the point when, after many disagreements, the men were no longer on speaking terms.

Not till October, 1800, did he go aboard the *Buffalo* and

allow Captain and Mrs. King, who had been reluctant guests of former friends for nearly six months, to take over Government House—which, for the first time in the colony's history, now really became a home.

The new Governor's Lady Mrs. Anna Josepha King, was a personality in her own right. Gay, energetic and kind, one of the first tasks she set herself was to care for the hundreds of neglected children—the 'broad-arrow babies'—running wild in Sydney. On Norfolk Island, King had seen to it that the waifs had whatever care and instruction it was possible to provide, and now his wife persuaded him to purchase Captain Kent's big house (built from the profits on those merinos). This became known as Mrs. King's Orphanage, where a hundred girls were taught to spin and write and 'prepare for virtuous wifehood'.

After two bachelor Viceroys, Government House now took for the first time its rightful place as the social centre of a colony so largely composed of the male sex. From their estates came the squires—Captain Foveaux, George Johnston, the redoubtable veteran of 1788 now transferred to the New South Wales Corps, and, of course, the Macarthurs with their children. Even Dr. D'Arcy Wentworth, who did not care for social gatherings, came to talk about the old days on Norfolk Island, and brought his son along. Young William was keenly disappointed that his friend Phillip had been left in England. The Macarthur boys talked of nothing but 'going home to school'; this was taken for granted in the case of the sons of the gentry. William's father, too, planned for him to go soon. But while the grown-ups spoke of England as 'home', for William New South Wales was his native land to which, he was certain, he would always wish to return.

At ten, he was a rather ungainly boy with an untidy thatch of auburn hair, and a cast in one eye did nothing to improve his appearance. Even as a small boy he had never been shy, and his self-confidence was now so remarkable that no one considered it strange to see him perched on a chair at grown-up gatherings, listening gravely to discussions on anything from Mrs. Marsden's latest baby to how much rum equalled the cost of a bushel of wheat or an Indian shawl.

Nothing much went on in the colony that he did not hear about but, unlike most of the inhabitants who viewed events only from their own standpoint, he got his news from all sides.

When Dr. Wentworth was transferred to Parramatta, William received an open invitation to Elizabeth Farm. As a family the Macarthurs were intellectually far above the usual run of colonial officials, and their sons were constrained to a certain amount of study to fit them for their schools in England. William fell hungrily on the bookshelves in the boys' room. He sat silent as the blistering tongue of John Macarthur castigated with scorn and contempt the efforts of some citizens—or Governor King himself—to oppose his will. Already he understood that Elizabeth Farm was the headquarters of Privilege, that his host was the acknowledged leader of what had come to be called the 'exclusive' class.

Everybody's immediate concern at that time were the activities of the Irish prisoners.

For centuries Ireland had been inflamed against British rule. In 1798 a rising of the 'United Irishmen' resulted in a

Captain Arthur Phillip
From a contemporary portrait bust

Sydney Cove, 1788: Captain Phillip and his officers drinking the royal toast after unfurling the flag on January 26th (now 'Australia Day')

From a painting by Algernon Talmage, R.A., at the Tate Gallery, London

stream of political prisoners being transported to New South Wales, who were giving as much trouble to Governor King as they had to his predecessor. It was impossible to treat them like ordinary felons. Many were educated men, some even of noble birth, and all of them gloried in their 'martyrdom', as did the 'Scottish martyrs' who were also exiled for their political opinions. Many broke out and escaped, one party even starting to 'walk to China', which they imagined to be on the other side of the mountains. So much did they preach rebellion that a 'Loyal Defence Association' of citizens was formed, drilled rather sarcastically by sergeants of the New South Wales Corps.

'Will there be a rising?' William asked one of them, Sergeant Knight, who happened to be a friend of his. It was a thrilling idea, but what could convicts do against trained soldiers?

'Maybe. But the poor devils would collapse in a night, and there'd be hangings and lashings to turn a man sick.'

The sergeant was troubled by something that went deeper than the trouble with the Irish—the moral atmosphere of the colony itself. Despite the good soldier's loyalty to his officers, Sergeant Knight had no illusions about the state to which their rule had brought New South Wales. He knew, moreover, as did everyone else, that the brain behind everything that went on, the great man of Sydney and Parramatta, was his own company commander.

By this time John Macarthur had grown far beyond the energetic young officer with the rapier mind whom Major Grose once described as 'an old head on young shoulders'. The rapier had given way to the bludgeon.

61

c

Opposition enraged him, conflict and intrigue were essential to him for their own sake, to feed the love of power which consumed him.

When Governor King issued the Order from the Duke of York, Commander-in-Chief of the Army, that 'all manner of traffic in spirits is forbidden to any person bearing the King's Commission in the Colony', a state of war came into existence, a war in which Macarthur was the brilliant superior of the kindly and harassed Viceroy.

'The Perturbator' was King's name for his arch-enemy. He knew that intrigue was going on all around him, the personal bickerings and hates of bored men living unnatural lives, all fanned and interwoven by the man who, King cried desperately, had 'the rapacity of a shark, and the cunning of a fox'. Then, suddenly, it seemed that he was saved, that his enemy had been delivered into his hands.

In May, 1802, Matthew Flinders, back in Sydney, wrote to his friend Kent: 'There is now Mrs. King and Mrs. Paterson and Mrs. Macarthur, for all of whom I have the greatest regard, who can scarcely speak to each other.' It was hardly surprising that the atmosphere was cool; for Mrs. Macarthur's husband was at sea—he had been sent to England by Mrs. King's husband for having wounded Mrs. Paterson's husband in a duel.

The events leading up to this scandal were, like everything concerning Macarthur, involved and complicated. For months he had been inciting the officers of the Corps against the Governor. When Colonel Paterson refused to call off his visits to Government House, Macarthur showed round a private letter to his wife in which Mrs. Paterson had suggested that Mrs. King was influencing her husband against Macarthur. His action broke two of the laws of honour—that private letters are sacred and that ladies' names must not be drawn into the differences of men. Into the ensuing storm of gossip broke the astounding news that the meek little colonel had challenged the captain to a duel, in the course of which the junior had, very unethically, gravely wounded his commanding officer!

On hearing the news, the Governor lost no time. 'One day that man will set the colony in a flame!' he had once cried despairingly to his wife. Macarthur was ordered into close arrest. 'My part, sir,' he wrote, all injured innocence, 'is obedience. *I* am the person who has been betrayed, who has been exulted over, who has been treated with the basest ingratitude and the blackest treachery.' Macarthur was not only always in the right; he also wanted to appear lofty and magnanimous under persecution.

Once Colonel Paterson was out of danger, the Governor made out an order for Captain John Macarthur 'to embark himself to England for trial'. But his mind was far from easy: who knew what tales that powerful man might not retail at home!

Before the trouble-maker's ship was due to sail, King wrote a private letter to the Under-Secretary of State:

Experience has convinced every man in the colony that there are no resources which art and cunning and a pair of basilisk eyes can afford that he does not put into practice to obtain any point he undertakes. Many instances of his diabolical spirit had shown itself before Governor Phillip left his colony, and since in many instances he has been the master-worker of the puppets he

English cartoon from the late eighteenth century

has set in motion. If Captain Macarthur returns here in any official character it should be that of Governor, as one half the colony already belongs to him, and it will not be long before he gets the other half.

CHAPTER V

'FOR THIS I WAS BORN'

IN 1800, Lieutenant Matthew Flinders had arrived in London with his beautiful charts of the coasts and islands of south-eastern New Holland, which he and George Bass had discovered over the last two years. Sir Joseph Banks, 'Sun of Science', now President of the Royal Society and the power behind the throne for the colony of New South Wales, received the young sailor with the greatest enthusiasm. Through his influence Matthew was offered the dream of his heart—a ship of his own for voyages in the cause of science, for mapping and charting the coasts of the country which in his logs and journals he had begun to call Australia, from 'Terra Australis Incognita' on old maps showing that mythical continent. At twenty-six he was promoted Captain—barring Nelson, the youngest ever to hold that rank.

Banks treated him like a favourite son; it seemed he could do no wrong. But in this he was to be sadly disappointed.

Rushing home to Lincoln on a brief leave, Matthew married Anne Chapple, his boyhood sweetheart. It was quite usual for a wife to sail in her husband's ship; he had written to her: 'Now I have accommodation on board *Investigator* in which my wife may, with love to assist her, make herself happy.' But the practice was frowned on by Sir Joseph Banks. Some gentlemen of the Admiralty, visiting the vessel while she lay in the Pool of London, chanced on the bride in her cabin. A few days later came the order that Mrs. Flinders must be put ashore, or the *Investigator* would sail with a different captain.

Heart-broken, the young husband pleaded, but Sir Joseph and the Admiralty were stony-hearted, and the dedicated explorer temporarily gave up his wife for his ship. 'For this I was born,' he said. 'If a plan for a voyage of discovery were to be read over my grave I would arise, awakened from the dead.' But he did not know then that he would not see his bride again for nearly ten years.

The First Lieutenant was his brother, Samuel Flinders, who turned out a bad choice. As midshipman went his young cousin, John Franklin, veteran of the Battle of Copenhagen, one day to make his own name as an Arctic explorer. While the *Investigator* was lying at Spithead she still had no Master; then in sailed the *Buffalo*, bringing angry ex-Governor Hunter home. Aboard was another friend, John Thistle, who had sailed on that first voyage round Van Diemen's Land—and the *Investigator* had her Master. Only the gay and gallant George Bass was missing. He had married the sister of Captain Waterhouse, and gone prospecting in the South Seas on his own account.

What became of Bass will never be known. After several trading voyages in his ship *Venus* he disappeared. Travellers reported having seen him in South America, and the unconfirmed legend is that he perished as a slave in the Peruvian silver mines.

In 1800, France and Britain were officially at war.

However, little fear was felt aboard the *Investigator* of an encounter with the enemy. Vessels engaged in scientific exploration carried passports signed by the Minister on the opposing side guaranteeing their safety. The document received by Flinders, worded in French, concerned the corvette *Investigator*, 334 tons, for a voyage of discovery into the Pacific with the object of extending human knowledge and furthering the progress of nautical science. The French Minister of Marine ordered all agents in the French colonies and ships to give every assistance to the commander and officers. 'It is however, understood that they will only obtain this assistance as long as they do not turn aside from their route or commit any hostile act against the French Government,' stated the document, a clause of much importance in view of what was to happen.

In addition to the crew, the company included an astronomer, a naturalist, two artists, a miner, and a gardener; also a folding conservatory to be filled with specimens which, everyone hoped, would one day grow in the Botanical Gardens at Kew.

On July 17th, 1800, the *Investigator* received her sailing orders for a voyage estimated to last four years. The course was via Madeira and the Cape of Good Hope. On December 7th, 1800, they sighted the Leeuwin, Australia's south-west corner, named Land of the Lioness in the old Dutch charts.

From that moment began the work of surveying and charting every mile of the tremendous outline of southern Australia—the name Flinders gave it, and by which he wished to have it called. Whenever possible, the ship

67

stood in close enough to see surf breaking on the beaches. Each day, a boat went ashore for Flinders to ascend the highest hill to take angles, a task that could mean a ten or twenty-mile walk while the artists and botanists busied themselves on their pursuits. Every evening he entered up his log. One entry reads:

The Indians do not seem desirous of communicating with strangers, they made signs to our gentlemen to return whence they came . . . but further on, they continued to visit us. I ordered a party of marines on shore to exercise in their presence. Their red coats and crossed belts were greatly admired. When they saw these beautiful red and white men, they absolutely screamed with delight . . . to the exercise they paid the most earnest silent attention. Several of them moved their hands involuntarily according to the motion, and the old man placed himself at the end of the rank with a short staff which he shouldered, presented, grounded as did the marines their muskets.

Flinders had a half-cask fitted to the masthead, where he spent all day, when not ashore, observing through his spyglass. A welcome change from salt pork for breakfast, dinner, and tea was the daily bag of strange birds, fish, even seals and sharks. A large island near the spot where Adelaide now stands was so crowded with kangaroos that the men gorged themselves with fresh meat. On this island they found a pelicans' dying-ground scattered with skeletons and bones, and that night Flinders waxed philosophical in his journal:

These islets in a hidden lagoon of an uninhabited island on an unknown coast near the antipodes of Europe . . . can anything be more consonant to the feeling of pelicans, if they have any, than quietly to resign their breath while surrounded by their progeny in the same spot where they first drew it? Alas for the pelicans, their golden age is past.

East of Kangaroo Island a sweep of coast is charted as Encounter Bay. The meeting that took place there on April 8th, 1802, was Flinders's first encounter with the French. Commander Charles Baudin of the *Géographe* could not have been more courteous; she and her sister ship, the *Naturaliste*, were also occupied in scientific survey. Flinders, always very correct, ordered out the boat for a formal visit. The two commanders exchanged passports and had a cordial talk, which ended in Flinders giving the Frenchman a copy of his chart and telling him what course he proposed to take. While on board, he was shocked to observe that the entire ship's company were so ill with scurvy that they could scarcely navigate the vessel.

On May 9th, the *Investigator* sailed triumphantly into Port Jackson 'with every single individual on deck, and officers and men in better health than on the day we sailed from Spithead, and not less in good spirits.'

What a contrast to the French ships which crawled in a month later! Out of a crew of 170, not more than 12 men were capable of doing their duty. Everything possible was done for their relief, the sick were received in hospital, and even some precious cattle were slaughtered to give them fresh meat.

In the midst of all this kindness extended to official enemies, news arrived of the signing of the Treaty of Amiens. The friends who joyfully celebrated the ending

69

of the war were not to know for what a short time the uneasy peace would last.

In Sydney everyone, from Governor King down to William Wentworth—now twelve years old, soon to sail off to school in England—hung on the words of the young man who had become a seasoned explorer. Authority sat easily on Flinders. The thin, tanned face was still quick to break into a smile, but when frowning in concentration he looked like a man of forty.

One 'discovery' he had made ten weeks too late; the huge inland sea on which now stands the city of Melbourne, which he had entered and partly surveyed. This immensely valuable harbour had been happened upon almost accidentally by Lieutenant Murray when cruising along the coast. Governor King decreed that it should be named Port Phillip.

To King, the company of Flinders at Government House was an especial pleasure. Here at last was someone free of contact with the feuds and jealousies that rent the colony. Though mercifully Macarthur was overseas, even without him the Rum Corps was driving the Governor nearly crazy. He was a humane and honest man with a dry sense of humour, but there was precious little in New South Wales for him to laugh about. The affairs of the settlement had really become too complex to be administered by one man, when those on whose aid he should have relied were arrayed against him.

The fundamental and prime cause of the colony's existence were still the convicts under sentence. Arrangements for their feeding and accommodation were frequently thrown into confusion by the arrival, unheralded, of hundreds more criminals, sowing much discontent among those who had already settled down. To the new-comers, the example of those set in authority over them scarcely encouraged the belief that the good life could only be achieved by keeping within the law.

The officers, both civil and military, had brought the rum trade to a fine art. They also held control over every shipload of goods entering the port, whether food, clothing, or tools. The only money negotiable outside New South Wales came from the British Treasury as pay for the army, or in bills for civil administration. Not a single item of food apart from official rations, no tool or implement got through to the public till members of the Ring had had their cut.

And what of the goods that trickled through to be bought by the general populace, the common soldiers, convicts on ticket-of-leave, and assigned servants? For them, barter was the rule, with rum as currency. *Rum*—the word covered every kind of poisonous fiery spirit, and of this, naturally, the officers fixed the rate of exchange.

While Flinders sailed north in the refitted *Investigator*, the Governor sought for a cure for the fever that inflamed his colony. As a result of the report sent home of the discovery of Port Phillip, a shipload of 300 convicts and settlers had been sent out in 1803 under Colonel David Collins, the former Judge-Advocate. After being tossed about in the dangerous Rip, where three tides meet off Port Phillip Heads, the party managed to pass through and make a landing on the eastern shore.

Today, the great city of Melbourne stretches its arms nearly fifty miles round each side of its inland sea. The spot where the little band landed is now part of a bracelet of holiday resorts, full of cars, camps and pic-nickers. But Collins, finding no water, considered the country hopeless for settlement. After struggling miserably for nearly a year, the party went back on board and set sail for Van Diemen's Land to join another tiny colony.

Two members of that company made their mark. The convict Fawkner fathered the man who would come back to help found the town of Melbourne. The other, Buckley, made his name a household word in the Australian language. When the North side of Port Phillip was first explored thirty-two years later, a bearded white man appeared in company with the natives. Stammering, almost unable to remember his own language, he told how he had lived during all those years as a member of the tribe. Today, Australians describe a risk taken against enormous odds as 'Buckley's chance'.

Now that Van Diemen's Land was known to be an island, it was the obvious place for expansion. In 1803, Lieutenant Bowen was sent to start a settlement on the lovely Derwent River, which eventually became the city of Hobart. In the North, Lieutenant Colonel Paterson organised Port Dalrymple near what is now Launceston.

Nearer Sydney, a punishment base on the Hunter River soon became a place of horror. Men called it the Coal River; today the town of Newcastle stands among mines, but in King's day, naked convicts, double-ironed, crept into holes in the cliff face to scrape out the coal. By the worst villains of all, unspeakable torture was endured as they stood all day, waist-deep in the surf, gathering oyster shells for lime. On bare backs already scored deep by the cat, the baskets dripped lime mixed with salt water.

For Flinders, the charting of the north coast was running less sweetly than the voyage round the Great Australian Bight had done. Despite her refit, the *Investigator* was leaking again. She had been picked out second-

Woodcut from a pamphlet published at Lincoln in the early 1800's, entitled 'A Complete Exposure of the Convict System, its Horrors, Hardships, and Severities, including an account of The Dreadful Sufferings of the Unhappy Captives'

hand from the English shipyards as was the custom; so had been Phillip's *Sirius*—so, if it came to that, had been Nelson's *Victory*—but a day-to-day, stop-and-go survey of the Barrier Reef was asking a great deal from the willing old craft. Flinders wrote: 'If a commander does not feel his nerves strong enough to thread the needle amongst the reefs while he directs the steerage from the masthead, I would strongly advise him not to approach this part of New South Wales.'

Up the coast they sailed, round the north point of Cape York into the deadening heat of the Gulf of Carpentaria. Few fish were caught, and a diet of salt pork, with little water, in that climate tested the strongest stomach. In addition to bad health, the state of the ship was on the Captain's mind, and he had cause to worry. And examination by the Master and the carpenter revealed that out of ten timbers, four were sound and the rest more or less rotten.

Flinders' face showed his concern: 'You mean if in any circumstances she went ashore, she would certainly go to pieces?'

The Master, an experienced man, nodded grimly: 'Sir, I have known several ships of this kind. When they start to rot, they go fast. In twelve months, there will scarce be a sound timber in her.'

'And in six months?' In half a year he could not finish the job, but he could get her back to Port Jackson with the journals and charts.

'In fine weather, and without accidents, she may run six months longer without too much risk,' was the verdict.

Not much risk! With the monsoon about to break and the storm weather in Torres Strait to face! Postponing further voyages of discovery, Flinders took the ship to Kepang in Timor, ending by sailing right round Australia to arrive in Port Jackson on June 9th, 1803, with almost the entire crew, including the commander, suffering from dysentery; one man died of it.

Humped over his desk, bandaged foot propped on a stool, Governor King pondered the draft of a letter. It was addressed to the Secretary of State, and contained his formal resignation. He had finished with New South Wales. Even after cancelling his annual order to London for thirty-six dozen bottles of port, his gout still plagued him day and night.

There was no pleasing the Government at home. They kept pressing him to stamp out the rum traffic; but when he had sent Major George Johnston home to be tried for contempt and disobedience of orders in that he had given spirits to his sergeant as part of the man's pay —and at an improper price, at that—the Major had returned unharmed in a ship loaded with his own livestock to furnish his estate at Annandale! The leniency was not unexpected, for the culprit was, King told himself grimly, under the patronage of His Grace the Duke of Northumberland.

And there was worse to come. King had news that John Macarthur, far from being cashiered and disgraced, was preparing to return to the colony as a civilian landowner with sheep from King George's Royal Merino Flock and official blessing in the shape of a grant of 10,000 acres to graze them on. What, the Governor asked himself unhappily, was the use of trying? Were it not for his excellent wife, Anna Josepha, he would think twice of struggling on at all. And now here was poor Flinders back with a ship rotting under his feet. He had written the most inspiring page in Australian history. The discovery of the Torres Strait between the mainland and New Guinea alone would have been worth the voyage, for it provided a new route to India. Now he must have a new ship to map the remaining quarter of the continent.

So rotten was the *Investigator* that the Master Builder and two other experts found it unnecessary to finish their examination.

'She's not worth repairing in any country,' summed up the commander of the *Porpoise*.

'How about your own ship, Captain?' asked King. 'Could the *Porpoise* stand up to survey work?'

The officer looked doubtful; so did Flinders. The young man looked terribly ill, thought King, almost in as bad a shape as his craft. With a flash of insight he realised that, apart from the two years' strain of command, Flinders' stomach had got along on salt pork and biscuit ever since he had started on that famous voyage under Captain Bligh at the age of sixteen. Almost his only time ashore had been among the meagre flesh-pots of Sydney Town. No wonder he suffered from a complaint he called 'the gravel'.

While the *Porpoise* was being surveyed, Flinders took a quiet holiday up the Hawkesbury. He returned to find that vessel pronounced far too decrepit for his purpose.

'There's only one way out,' the Governor told him. 'The *Porpoise* can take you home. Sail as a passenger and get a new ship to finish your survey.'

So Matthew Flinders and his crew set out, with Sir Joseph's precious greenhouse on deck full of specimens, and the priceless charts and journals stowed in the cabin. With the *Porpoise* in convoy sailed two East Indiamen, the *Cato* and the *Bridgewater*.

On August 17th, 1803, disaster struck. Coming up to the Barrier Reef a shout rang out, 'BREAKERS AHEAD!' The ship was forced off its course to strike a coral reef, taking a fearful heel-over as the mast was carried away and the bottom stoved in. The two other ships almost collideed, and the *Cato*, giving way, struck a reef herself and fell over on her side. The *Bridgewater* sailed on, leaving the shipwrecked mariners to their fate. (As if in retribution, after leaving Bombay the *Bridgewater* was lost with all hands.)

The calamity took place at dusk, and a terrible night was passed. But at sunrise, by amazing luck, a dry sand-bank appeared half a mile distant, and eventually ninety-four half-naked men set foot on what they christened 'Wreck Reef' with a quantity of salvaged provisions and two and a half hogsheads of water.

At a council-of-war, Flinders was chosen to take the six-oar cutter—H.M.S. *Hope*, they named her—and row back 63 leagues to Sydney for help. His account of this feat is one of the classic understatements of all time:

The reader has perhaps never gone 250 leagues (674 miles) at sea in an open boat or along a strange coast inhabited by savages. But should he recollect the eighty officers and men upon Wreck Reef and how important our arrival was to their safety, and the saving of the charts, journals and papers of the *Investigator*'s voyage, he may have some idea of the pleasure we felt, but particularly myself, at entering our destined port. . . . With Captain Park I went immediately to wait upon H. E. Governor King, whom we found at dinner with his family. A razor had not passed over our faces from the time of the shipwreck, and the surprise of the Governor was not little at seeing two persons thus appear whom he supposed to be many leagues on their way to England. But so soon as he was convinced of the truth of the vision before him and learned the melancholy cause, an involuntary tear started from the eye of friendship and compassion and we were received in the most affectionate manner.

Now the problem of getting Flinders away was even more difficult than before. There was no ship in Port Jackson for Europe, only the *Rollo*, China-bound. Flinders, passionately anxious to finish his survey, twice frustrated, felt his whole future was at stake . . . and waiting at home was his bride of nearly three years ago.

'If I had *any* ship I'd sail her home,' he cried desperately. King remembered that there was a ship called the *Cumberland*; then he smiled at the absurdity of it: a tiny schooner of 29 tons, Sydney-built, scarcely more than a ferry-boat. But the *Cumberland* Flinders took, accepting rather unwillingly some despatches King pressed on him at the last moment.

'Her performance on the way to Wreck Reef,' wrote Flinders, 'did not lead me to think favourably of the vessel in which I had undertaken a voyage half round the world . . . but the pleasure of rejoining my companions made this one of the happiest moments of my life.' He took on volunteers to work the crazy little vessel, and on October 10th, 1803, the *Cumberland* sailed from Wreck Reef.

For a mariner sailing across the Indian Ocean, a natural port of call would be Mauritius, or *l'Ile de France* as it was called by its owners. But Governor King had strongly advised him to avoid it, saying 'there are dangerous hurricanes in those parts'. It was true enough that there was always a chance of encountering a hurricane in the tropics, and *l'Ile de France* lay almost exactly on the line of Capricorn; but it also lay dead opposite Australia's western coast, wide open and defenceless against attack. At peace or not, the less contact between that continent and the French, the better, thought Governor King anxiously.

CHAPTER VI

THE HERO OF
THE FLEECE

IN New South Wales, the great excitement of the year 1805 was the return of John Macarthur.

The 'perturbator's' trip to England had been a master-stroke of fate, both for his own fortunes and for those of Australia. Few defendants ever departed for trial in better spirits. The fact that his ship was dismasted in a storm might have been accounted unfortunate were it not that, on putting into Amboyna for a new vessel, he fell in with a young gentleman named Robert Farquhar who was also returning to England under a cloud.

The small East Indian island of Amboyna has a larger place in history than is warranted by its size. In 1623, a dispute about its ownership resulted in a massacre, when ten Englishmen were executed in a trumped-up charge of conspiring against the Dutch Governor. In 1796, the British captured it. Now it was soon to revert to its former owners, partly owing to the inexperience of the British Governor, called 'the Resident'. Though this gentle-man, at the tender age of twenty-three, could scarcely be blamed for bungling a job which he only held by virtue of being the son of Sir Walter Farquhar, Surgeon to the Prince of Wales, he had been recalled in disgrace to answer for his misdeeds. Macarthur's characteristic advice that 'attack is the best means of defence' brought him a valuable patron in the days to come. On arrival in London, Sir Walter Farquhar received his son's adviser with the greatest cordiality, inviting him to stay at his house indefinitely, and for many years Macarthur had cause to be grateful for the chance that had taken him to Amboyna.

The Government, worried out of its mind about Napoleon glaring across the Channel from the cliffs of Boulogne, had no time to waste on young men's year-old peccadilloes. All Lord Hobart, now in charge of colonial affairs, knew was that New South Wales was an infernal nuisance with its constant wrangling and demands for money. A sharp note was sent off to Governor King that he would do better to settle such local matters himself without bothering Ministers with better things to do.

To London society Macarthur, introduced by his new patron, was an intriguing mixture of the handsome officer and the wild colonial boy. But drawing-room dalliance held no attraction for him; ambition drove him on. He had brought samples of his fleeces, and it was a case of the right man in the right place at the right time.

Ever since the invention of the flying shuttle and the spinning jenny, there had been improvements in the making of cloth. The new war which was flaring up brought a demand for uniforms just when Spanish wool had become unobtainable. Manufacturers fell on Macarthur's neck. He was allowed to buy merinos from the King's own flock. Lord Camden, now Colonial Secretary, granted him five thousand acres to be taken up on his return, with another five thousand to come wherever he might select them. His resignation from the army was accepted, to enable him to devote himself full-time to his plans for the creation of a fine wool industry in New South Wales.

On June 12th, 1805, John Macarthur Esq. sailed triumphantly through Sydney Heads aboard his own ship, the *Argo*, his figurehead of the Golden Fleece shining at the prow, the royal merinos pushing their noses curiously from the pens. The once penniless officer had been transformed into a rich grazier with powerful friends at Court, prospective owner of the famous cow-pastures where the herds of wild cattle, descendants of the runaways of 1788, now grazed undisturbed. In his train came his nephew Hannibal, his daughter Elizabeth, a new business associate, Mr. Davidson, and two expert woolsorters.

Governor King accepted the situation with grim humour. He wrote an account of the incident to Sir Joseph Banks (no friend of Macarthur) describing 'the arrival of the hero of the fleece, which, though long expected, caused a little sensation', and invited his former tormentor to Government House. He could afford to regard the return with detachment, since his own resignation had at last been accepted, and it would fall to his successor to cope with the future machinations of the troublemaker. That the latter would not remain for long in the background was certain. He was a man to whom controversy was the breath of life, and his new success had undoubtedly inflated still further his monstrous egotism. King almost wished he could be there to see the fun.

However, it seemed that the 'hero of the fleece' planned for the moment to devote himself to his home and his flocks. So peaceful were the relations between Government House and Elizabeth Farm that later that year Mrs. Macarthur and her family actually stayed several weeks with the Kings.

Perhaps it was during that visit that the seeds were sown of the romance that culminated years later by the marriage of Hannibal Macarthur and Maria King, uniting the two families. The Governor's Lady, struggling with her husband's gout and the meagre vice-regal housekeeping, might have enjoyed a peep into the future: at herself thirty years on, in Maria's lovely house on the Parramatta River, surrounded by Macarthur's grandchildren playing with their cousins—the seven sons of Vice-Admiral (retired) Phillip Parker King, famous for completing the explorations of Matthew Flinders.

The news from Flinders, received nearly a year late, saddened the Kings' last days at Government House.

As all the colony soon knew, the miserable *Cumberland* had proved so leaky that Flinders had been forced to put in at the French island of Mauritius against his will. He did not know that war between the two countries had flared up again. What happened there was hard to believe.

In the interval between the wars, the Governor, Captain Decaen, had been appointed Captain-General of all French possessions East of the Cape of Good Hope. With his newly-married, beautiful young wife he sailed Indiaward to lord it among the rajahs, arriving just after the Peace of Amiens had broken down. Without ceremony the couple had been bundled out of India by the British, and the brilliant bubble shrivelled into the Governorship of the little *l'Ile de France*, otherwise called Mauritius.

Decaen's wounded pride sorely needed a scapegoat, and here was a self-styled English Captain-explorer delivered into his hands. True, there was a passport, but this was made out for a Captain Flinders commanding the corvette *Investigator* of 334 tons, with a crew of 83 men plus 5 scientists. His story of shipwreck was unconvincing, to put it mildly. Was it conceivable that any Governor, even of a small penal colony, would allow an important scientific officer to sail half-way round the world in a leaky 29-ton schooner no larger than a ferry boat?

The indignant Flinders was detained and his ship searched, to reveal Governor King's letters to Whitehall.

Decaen flourished the passport: 'So, Captain Flandaire! If, as you say, you sail under the conditions of this document, how comes it that you carry the despatches which are strictly forbidden by its terms?'

Useless for Flinders to protest that when he left New South Wales, France and England were still at peace. His doom was sealed by a trivial incident. After an interview in which he had been called a spy, a liar, and an imposter, Flinders received a message inviting him to dinner with the Governor and his wife.

'Inform Captain Decaen that I have already dined,' the hungry prisoner replied haughtily.

Whether or not the invitation had been issued to gratify Madame's curiosity, the refusal decided Flinders' fate. Despite the efforts of friends, the protests of influential men and societies over half the world, even pleas to Napoleon himself, he was kept prisoner in Mauritius for six and a half years, his health and career ruined and his spirit almost broken by continued frustration. Almost the bitterest blow was to learn that the French explorers whom he had thought his friends had published books claiming a large part of his discoveries as their own.

When he reached England, nearly ten years after leaving it in the *Investigator*, his old complaint, 'the gravel', was slowly killing him. He was only thirty-seven, but Anne wrote that he looked a man of seventy. In poverty, nursed devotedly by his wife, he worked for four years on his great book, *A Voyage to Terra Australis*, (even then Sir Joseph Banks would not sanction the name 'Australia'). Matthew Flinders never saw his book in print, for he died on the day of publication, July 19th, 1814.

All through March, the rain had fallen without a break. Each year the Hawkesbury River swelled dangerously, but in 1806 the water rose to a raging torrent. Soon it would flood over the banks, menacing the farms on the fertile land that held the hopes of emancipated convicts and free settlers who had sunk their savings and years of backbreaking toil into their acres. On Black Friday, families found water lapping their beds. They fled to rooftops, to wheatstacks, into the trees. The morning of March 22nd broke on a scene of horror all around.

Houses had collapsed; furniture, horses, pigs, and cows were all swept down on the swirling waters. It was the greatest disaster that had ever befallen the colony. Andrew Thompson, ex-convict Chief Constable, was among those who went round with boats rescuing people from housetops and rafts. The flood waters had transformed the Hawkesbury settlement into a sea measuring thousands of acres.

As well as the market gardens which should have supplied Sydney and Parramatta, thousands of bushels of grain were destroyed, not to mention the cows and hogs, the goats and fowls. For a long time, the colony had been feeding itself; now it had to tighten its belt again.

The effect of the flood was not only physical but moral. The price of grain asked by those who still had it soared sky-high. The ruined settlers lost the urge to work: 'What's the use?' they asked. The distress was still rampant when Governor Bligh took over from the defeated King.

Captain William Bligh, R.N., was always in the news. As a boy, he had sailed with the legendary Captain Cook. His two voyages round the world in an attempt to transplant breadfruit from Otaheite to the West Indies made him a legend and gave him the nickname of 'Breadfruit Bligh'. His feat of navigating an open boat, cast loose by the mutineers of the *Bounty*, four thousand miles across the Pacific to Timor set his name amongst the great navigators of all time. After the Nore mutiny of 1797 he was commended for his sternness of action, and Nelson had publicly thanked him after the Battle of Copenhagen.

Breadfruit Bligh, Bounty Bligh—now it was to be Bligh of Botany Bay. Those who knew his reputation remarked, 'Now that troublesome colony will be brought to heel!' Some added: 'They've got what they deserve—poor devils!' Just prior to his appointment he had himself emerged from a court martial; he was acquitted, but with the advice that he should restrain the violence and profanity of his language. Though he was recommended by Sir Joseph Banks, it would have been hard to find a man less fitted for the tricky task of governing the New

South Wales of 1806. Accustomed to supreme authority on the quarterdeck, he demanded instant obedience to his colourfully-worded orders, heartily despising such land-lubbers' qualities as tact and diplomacy.

Like many public tyrants, Bligh was a devoted family man. His wife could not face the long sea voyage, so his favourite among their six daughters had accompanied him to act as the Governor's Lady. Mary Putland was a beautiful young woman whose high temper matched her father's own. She came with her ailing husband, Lieutenant Putland; he was suffering from consumption, and it was hoped the sunny climate would improve his health—but he was dying, and nothing could save him.

With Bligh, physical well-being was a passion. To his ships' companies his orders had always been 'Keep fit . . . or else!' He had learned from Captain Cook that certain foods helped to prevent scurvy, and he was perfectly capable of ordering a man twenty lashes for not eating his prescribed limes or lemons. Dancing was good exercise in a small ship: so for half an hour a day a fiddle was ordered to be played while the Captain goaded his hot and thirsty men to 'Dance, damn you!' until they fell to the deck in sheer exhaustion. The martinet was no less strict with himself, and consequently his health was excellent, though his stocky figure had grown thicker with the years, and he sometimes seemed about to choke with the violence of the words issuing from his throat in fits of rage.

Most naval officers with large families are in financial straits; Bligh planned to take up land and start farming as a profitable sideline. On hearing this proposal, Philip

King gave a grim laugh. With a young family of his own, how often had he regretted the law forbidding Viceroys to grant themselves land!

'Confound it, man!' exploded Bligh, '*I* am not the Viceroy, *you* are! What's to prevent you making a grant to me, a private citizen? And in due course,' he added with a wink, 'there could be no possible objection to my returning the favour to Captain King, R.N. Eh? Eh?'

Bligh named his property Camperdown after his favourite battle. King, sardonic to the end, later called the 790 acres granted in his wife's name simply Thanks.

The blustering old salt proved an excellent organiser. Above all things he prized order and efficiency, and it was with considerable pleasure that he plunged into the task of bringing relief to the ruined settlers on the Hawkesbury, riding on horseback to the outlying homesteads and stumping around the farms. The luckless smallholders, whether poor freemen or ex-convicts, were accustomed to rough language, and the Governor's interest was both unexpected and appreciated. Among Bligh's good ideas was the free grinding of corn, with every eleventh bushel made over to the settlers' relief fund.

Feeling ran high against those unaffected by the floods who were profiteering from the food shortage, particularly Macarthur, who arrogantly refused to slaughter his precious wool-bearing sheep to turn them into mutton stew. The fact that Macarthur had taken it upon himself to sign an Address of Welcome on behalf of the free settlers, annoyed them intensely, to the point of repudiating him in a new Address as 'an unfit person to step forward on such an occasion, as we may chiefly attribute a rise in the price of mutton to his withholding the large flock of wethers he now has to make any price he may choose to demand'. In this Address the settlers set out what they considered would be a fair set of rules for trading, and a month later they thanked Bligh for 'having rescued them from their dreadful crisis of general calamity'.

Bligh had thus set out to carry on the Government's policy of running the colony as a settlement of small farmers, and to his own mind this was proceeding successfully. In the following year he reported home that 'industrious settler farmers are raising their heads and becoming independent of their creditors'; that he himself was 'polite and attentive to everyone, and gratifying them with every means in my power'; that 'this sink of iniquity Sydney is improving in its manners and its concerns'.

If all the inhabitants of that 'sink of iniquity' had been humble workmen, life for the Governor would have been rewarding indeed.

For William Bligh, the performance of his duty was his simple religion. Duty was white, disobedience was black, and he admitted no confusing shading in between. His duty was to enforce the law; but in New South Wales, what *was* the law?

Under the incorruptible Phillip, David Collins, the Marine Judge Advocate, had functioned on commonsense lines, with no appeal except to the Governor. But in his day there were no emancipists, no free rich settlers, no officers bent on cleaning up a fortune. Once the New South Wales Corps led by Grose and Macarthur was in control, the law was what they chose to make it. The Bench of the Criminal Court consisted of six officers of the Corps, presided over by Richard Atkins, Esq., Judge Advocate.

Mr. Atkins was an incubus which each Governor in turn had passed on to his successor—a dissipated drunkard to whom his extremely high-born relatives in England thankfully paid large sums to keep him on the other side of the world. That such a man, with neither moral standards nor legal knowledge, should hold such a position was a scandal, but the power of the names behind him was such that no Governor dared displace him. Ten years of bitter warfare had raged between him and John Macarthur, both by the spoken word and by letters that read as though written in corrosive acid. Though Bligh was shocked by the way of life of the character he described as 'a disgrace to human jurisprudence', the two were drawn together by a common hatred of the man Bligh soon named the Archfiend.

CHAPTER VII

THE RUM REBELLION

AT the outset of Bligh's reign, relations between Government House and Elizabeth Farm were on the surface friendly enough. The two families visited each other, even dined together. But with two such strong characters in a small community, discord was inevitable. The first clash came when Macarthur brought up the subject of the second five thousand acres promised to him by Lord Camden. His Excellency flew into a violent passion.

"What have I to do with your sheep, sir?" he bellowed. 'Are you to have such flocks and herds as no man ever heard of? You have got five thousand acres, sir, in the finest situation in the country, but by God, sir, you shan't keep it!'

Bligh was an erupting volcano, his opponent a man of ice who coldly pointed out that the land had been granted by order of the Privy Council and the Secretary of State.

But the Governor continued to rant and bluster. 'Damn the Secretary of State!' he shouted. 'He commands at home, *I* command here!' This scene, which took place in the presence of ex-Governor King and several other officers, was an example of what Dr. Arnold—a naval surgeon who was well used to the behaviour of senior officers—noted of Bligh at the end of his reign: that he 'overpowered and affrighted every person who might have dealings with him, expecting from all a deference and submission that the proudest despot would covet'.

He would certainly not obtain submission from John Macarthur. However, relations were not definitely severed until July, 1807, when the magnate Macarthur considered himself unjustly treated in a lawsuit over some wheat, after which personal contact between them was broken off. It was a case of the irresistible force meeting the (as Bligh thought) immovable body, though the head-on collision was yet to come.

The battle was more than a personal feud between two outsize personalities. It was a struggle between two systems: a penal colony under autocratic rule, and a society devoted to the pursuit of individual wealth. Bligh might issue edicts forbidding the sale of rum—they went into pigeon-holes. Whenever trouble boiled up, Macarthur's name always seemed to appear in the background. He was the storm centre of a series of firework displays which blazed the trail to the final explosion, such as the case of his brewing-still which Bligh decreed should be taken to the Government store from the ship in which it arrived, but which somehow came into Macarthur's possession after all, though minus its heads and screws.

All this time Bligh was convinced that he was personally popular and in complete control of the colony. Everyone was happy, he wrote home, except for a small group of traders whose graft he was successfully stamping out—this at a time when Mr. Mann, lately secretary to Governor King, warned Palmer the Commissary that the inhabitants of Sydney were 'in a state of great fright', and unless they were conciliated, he thought 'a revolution would surely happen'. And then the 'pipes' began to appear.

The pipe or lampoon was a favourite weapon of the times. Witty and usually scurrilous verses, written on rolls of paper, were planted in inns and grog-shops, to be passed from hand to hand amid loud laughter. Governor King had suffered from them, now it was Bligh's turn—there was always a tale-bearer eager to carry their contents to the victim. Bligh soon learned of the latest one circulating in Sydney:

> O tempora! O mores! Is there no CHRISTIAN in New
> South Wales
> to put a stop to the tyranny of Governor Bligh?'

The memory of the *Bounty* was graven deep on the soul of Captain Bligh. Revenge against the mutineers who had cast him loose had for years been the ruling passion of his life. Above all, their ringleader, Fletcher Christian, had been the one to haunt his bitterest dreams. He had seen two mutinies, at Otaheite and on the Nore. Never again! grimly swore William Bligh.

The latest embroilment with Macarthur had been over a convict who had escaped in one of his ships. Wrangling had dragged on for some weeks when suddenly all Sydney was agog with exciting news. The Chief Constable of Parramatta, Mr. Oakes, had delivered at Elizabeth Farm a letter requesting Mr. Macarthur to appear in Sydney next morning at 10 o'clock 'to show cause for his conduct'. Macarthur replied in writing that any information required could be had from the two police officials on board the vessel.

Next evening Mr. Oakes was back again, a little worried, for he bore with him a warrant for the arrest of

93

John Macarthur, signed by the Bench of Magistrates. The family was on the point of retiring for the night, and a scene of considerable violence ensued. Mr. Macarthur was very angry indeed. Eventually the messenger was handed the following note:

Mr. Oakes,

You will inform the persons who sent you here with the warrant you have now shewn me, and given me a copy of, that I never will submit to the horrid tyranny that is attempted until I am forced; that I consider it with scorn and contempt, as I do the persons who have directed it to be executed.

Nevertheless, Macarthur—persuaded no doubt by his family—duly appeared in Sydney next morning, when a bail for £1,000 was put up by his friends. The following day he was brought before the Bench of Magistrates, and was committed for trial before the Criminal Court in one month's time. On what charge? The defendant was not informed, an omission which gave him full scope for playing his favourite rôle of injured innocent during the four weeks when, as an offender on bail, he busied himself in preparing for his trial. Private information had led him to fear that the charge might even be for treason, and he had good reason to be afraid in the light of the enemies arrayed against him.

Bligh's chief adviser at this time was an ex-convict lawyer who had somehow insinuated himself into Viceregal favour. George Crossley's case history included perjury, forgery and a piquant story that he had once placed a fly in the mouth of a corpse while guiding the dead man's hand to sign his Will, swearing later that 'life had been in him at the time' . . . This sly old wretch, who certainly knew more about the seamy side of the law than anyone else in New South Wales, was a strange counsellor for the Governor. As far as Atkins, his other adviser, was concerned, Bligh had described him three months earlier in a letter to the Colonial Secretary as 'weak and a blabber, a drunkard, ridiculous and in legal matters subservient to private inclination'.

The trial was fixed for the eve of January 26th, 1808, this being the twentieth anniversary of the landing at Sydney Cove, in which Major George Johnston, grizzled Commandant of the Corps, had taken part. On the evening of the 24th, a convivial gathering took place. Among those present on that Sunday evening were the six members of the Rum Corps who would next day sit in judgement on their ex-brother officer: Macarthur's son Edward, his nephew Hannibal, and his partner Garnham Blaxcell. The defendant himself, teetotaller and dyspeptic, did not join the party but stalked about the town pondering his defence, so that next day he was perhaps the only man in court not suffering from the effects of 'the morning after'. Major Johnston himself was not even able to attend the trial. On emerging from the convivial gathering he had stepped into his chaise and driven off in fine style, only to be thrown out by his horse which, sensing the uncertainty of the hand holding the reins, proceeded to kick the equipage to bits. So on this important occasion the Rum Corps' Commanding Officer was confined to bed, nursing his bruises and a very sore right arm.

The whole sequence of the events of January 25th and 26th, 1808, reads like a chapter from *Alice in Wonderland*. The Monday was a hot and sultry day. Into the small room, packed with as many of the interested citizens of Sydney as could thrust themselves into the space allotted to the public, clanked the six scarlet-coated officers to take their seats on the Bench. Following them as President came the Judge-Advocate; but before he in his turn could take the oath and kiss the Book, an interruption came from the Prisoner at the Bar. John Macarthur wished to register a protest.

'Be silent!' thundered Mr. Atkins; but Captain Kemp, the senior military member, told the defendant he might speak. Everyone began talking at once, with the voice of the Judge Advocate shouting above the din: 'No court! No court!' At this, the crowd of onlookers began pushing their way out to discuss the proceedings with greater freedom in the open air. But 'Stay where you are, we ARE a court!' cried Captain Kemp, while Atkins, choking with rage, threatened to charge everyone present with contempt.

Order being partially restored, the prisoner began to read his protest in a voice whose cold disdain contrasted strongly with the heated atmosphere of the rest of the court. His objections were based on the fact that he had been brought to trial unacquainted with the charges against which he would have to defend himself. In such circumstances he considered it prudent and 'a piece of justice which I owed to the community' to protest against Richard Atkins Esq. being appointed to sit as Judge on a trial in which he was so much interested; he went on to make a number of reflections on the character of the Judge Advocate, which so far had not been exhibited in the glaring light of day. This speech was important in being the first open criticism of Government rule in Australian history, the first challenge without fear of consequences. It blasted Richard Atkins right out of the courtroom and up the hill to Government House to ask the Viceroy what he should do next.

All day, messengers rushed back and forth between Bligh and the Officers of the Court, till at five o'clock everyone adjourned for refreshment, remanding the prisoner on bail. At nine next morning, however, two constables arrived at his home. Despite the fact that the arrest of a prisoner on bail is against all legal procedure, they took him into custody and bore him off to the common jail in full view of all the rag, tag and bobtail of Sydney. Apart from its disgusting conditions, the common jail was a place of alarming danger for John Macarthur, for he had been the means of landing many of its inmates in that stinking spot. So he had cause to be grateful to the jailer who, perhaps with an eye to his own future safety, whispered that he had slipped a cutlass into the cell so that he could defend himself in case of need.

The news of Macarthur's arrest ran through the town like a fire, spreading general consternation, for who might be the next one cast within those unsavoury portals on some unspecified charge? Crowds quickly assembled outside the jail and round the courthouse, and the feeling of riot was in the air. Fanning the flames of excitement came the tidings that, on the insistence of Mr. Atkins, the Governor had ordered the magistrates to issue a summons to each of the Judges of the previous day's court. The news threw them into consternation in their turn; for all they knew, Bligh might accuse *them* of treason, for which crime the mediaeval penalty of being hanged, drawn and quartered still remained on the Statute Book.

An envoy had galloped off to Annandale to inform the Commanding Officer, Major Johnston, of the turn events had taken. Immediately the Major rose from his bed of pain to drive, not to Government House but to the Barracks, where he arrived to find the leading citizens and civil and military officers assembled, who begged him to do something to dispel the general alarm. What he did was to order the drums to beat to call the soldiers together. Major Johnston then took an action which sealed his fate. He wrote out to the Chief Jailer an order for the release of John Macarthur, signing under his name the words 'Lieutenant Governor'. The officer commanding the Garrison did in fact hold that position *ex officio*; but to sign such an order, which expressly countermanded the command of the Governor himself, was to usurp the authority of His Majesty's representative—in a word, mutiny!

Thousands of words have been written on the Bligh-Macarthur clash by historians almost as fiercely opposed as were the two men themselves. One side portrays Macarthur as the demon with no redeeming feature, pitted against a noble (though short-tempered) and selfless administrator, the idol of the settlers. To the other school of thought, the qualities of the two opponents are almost exacly reversed, and partisan and official records can be quoted at length to prove either side right.

However, there is no argument about what actually happened when Macarthur was triumphantly rescued from jail to become the leading spirit of the rebellion. Among the historical documents of New South Wales is a demand for the Governor's arrest, drafted in Macarthur's own handwriting with the violence of his anger showing in the pressure on the quill, and beneath it the signatures of Blaxland, D'Arcy Wentworth, and many others who thronged around under the blazing January sun.

Governor Bligh, imagining that for the moment he could relax after his wearying day, was sitting at dinner with his daughter and some of his intimate supporters. To them was borne the sound of music; looking out of the window the Governor saw an incredible sight. Up the hill from the barracks came three hundred soldiers, colours flying, band playing 'The British Grenadiers'. In the lead marched Major Johnston himself, right arm still in a sling, while the left grasped his sword. In the rear came the mob of Sydney, most of them having taken drink, and determined not to miss the fun.

The Governor's first reaction was to rush upstairs and change into his uniform, while his daughter ran to the gate, trying to prevent the mutineers from entering the house. Though slight of figure, Mrs. Putland had inherited her father's temper, and it was not unknown for plates and other objects to be hurled through the air at Government House. But her eloquence had no effect. She was respectfully but firmly moved aside. Up the avenue marched the troops, and Major Johnston led a select party through the main entrance to confront Captain Bligh.

But the Governor was nowhere to be found, neither downstairs nor in his bedroom. Strewn about his study, however, was something even more interesting—official papers dropped from the armfuls he had swept up before making his way upstairs. The merest glance showed these to be of entrancing interest to the officers of the Rum Corps, consisting as they did of Bligh's reports and comments on their action and personal characters. Time

99

passed quickly as the interested parties settled down to read these damning documents. Meanwhile, the soldiers ransacked the house; what with the heat and the excitement it was thirsty work, but refreshment was readily available from the viceregal stores.

Still no trace could be found of His Excellency. Had he escaped by a rear door? Out went the posse through the outhouses and grounds—even the shed in which the *Sydney Gazette* was produced by ex-convict George Howe. But the sentries swore no one had passed them, and back they trooped to search every nook and cranny on the first floor—even the loft, out of which in his zeal painfully fell Lieutenant Laycock, to provide the only casualty of the 'revolution'.

But the quarry was cornered at last. A soldier opened a small door and let out a whoop of triumph. There, in a tiny room that held nothing but a bed, was His Excellency.

According to his own story, he had 'spent two hours deliberating what could be done for the restoration of his authority', and destroying such papers as he had been able to snatch up. These, he asserted, he was trying to conceal under the bed when he was found, but 'hiding under it' was what the soldier said, a tale that seemed borne out when he was escorted downstairs 'with dust on his lapels, feathers on his coat and bed-flue on his rear portions'. Whether the story was true or false, it was gleefully repeated all over the colony and for years enchanted Bligh's many enemies on land and sea.

That night, 'topical transparencies' decorating the windows were all the rage from Sydney to Parramatta, revelry held sway, bonfires blazed, bells rang. Within a week, John Macarthur, the martyred victim who had organised the whole rebellion, temporarily became ruler of New South Wales under the newly invented title of 'Colonial Secretary' while the deposed legal Governor was 'held in custody for his own protection'.

The result was inevitable. The Home Authorities, when eventually the ship bearing the news made port, would not tolerate a revolution, however extenuating the circumstances might be. Every man involved who held the King's Commission was summoned to London, and most of those not summoned hastened there of their own volition, for who knew what strange tales might be told by people anxious to save their reputations? Those who made most haste were the rebel faction, for the men who had backed the Governor could afford to wait and see which way the cat would jump; and what with the Peninsular War and King George III going mad again, more than three years went by before the accused officer at last faced his judges.

In the London of 1811 the court-martial of Major George Johnston which had been postponed so many times that it seemed as if it was never going to happen at all, was an unimportant event. The accused major and his brother-in-crime, John Macarthur, had landed in England to find that the latter's eldest son had the ground well prepared. Edward Macarthur, now a war veteran, had been visiting all the right people and drumming up some old New South Wales stalwarts, of whom there were by now quite a number. Everything looked promising for the defence. However, nothing could be done until Captain Bligh arrived; when at last he did bring his cohorts of witnesses, all the lobbying had to begin all over again.

D•

John Macarthur, who had confidently expected to be sailing home in a matter of months, worried and fumed himself into a state of mind which was fatal to his weak digestion. His health, never good, broke down and from then on got steadily worse.

Among the many who asked favours from Macarthur for old time's sake was D'Arcy Wentworth, who wrote from Sydney suggesting that perhaps he could use his influence to secure for his son, William, a position with the East India Company. The boy, 'a very pleasing lad' as Macarthur described him to his wife, had learned all that his latest tutor, Dr. Crombie of Greenwich, could teach him. However nothing came of the idea for a post with 'John Company', as the East India Company was jokingly called, after John Bull; and young William decided that for the time being he would return to his native land. With him went his brother, D'Arcy Junior, who had also been pursuing his education in England.

CHAPTER VIII

THE KINDLING OF AMBITION

WHEN William Wentworth had first arrived in England at the age of thirteen, he already knew a good deal about the penal colony of New South Wales and how its foundations and development stemmed from the changing conditions in the old world. During the next seven of his most formative years the growing boy saw the whole might of Britain being strained almost to breaking point in the struggle against Napoleon, while the master of the Continent strove to starve the country by his naval blockade. The war in Spain, though finally successful, drained Britain's resources of money and men, and the agony went on till Napoleon met his defeat at Waterloo in the year before Wentworth returned to New South Wales.

He found the colony scarcely recognisable as the place he had left as a budding schoolboy seven years earlier.

Colonel Lachlan Macquarie, the new Viceroy who had taken office on New Year's Day, 1810, was a very different kind of man from any of his predecessors. Despite their preoccupation with Napoleon—or perhaps because of it—the British Government had been jolted into some alarm by the news of the rebellion in New South

Wales. Ever since the French Revolution, the ruling classes of England had been obsessed with the fear that the dreadful infection of rebellion might spread across the Channel. This led to the arrest and transportation of any person suspected of holding dangerous ideas about the *Rights of Man*; one man had been sentenced to seven years' transportation for merely possessing a copy of Tom Paine's famous treatise.

In consequence, shiploads of 'politicals' arrived in New South Wales to add their seditious notions to the fiery sentiments of the Scottish and Irish 'Martyrs', engendering an atmosphere of rebellion which would have called forth from any of the old-time Governors an orgy of punishment at the flogging post and the gallows.

However, the British Government, with an unusual flash of insight, decided that perhaps supremacy on the quarter-deck did not provide the ideal training for the Governorship of a troublesome colony. Perhaps, they mused, a soldier would bring a surer touch to this tricky post. A youngish veteran of America and the Indies, Brigadier Miles Nightingall, was appointed to replace Bligh; the New South Wales Corps was to be disbanded, and the 73rd Regiment was to replace it under its commander, Lieutenant-Colonel Lachlan Macquarie.

But Brigadier Nightingall, having no relish for the rôle of prison warder, pleaded rheumatism in his right arm and declined the honour. Lieutenant-Colonel Macquarie, since he was in any case 'to be transported', as he wryly put it, applied for the Governorship and was duly appointed. Neither he nor his men had much enthusiasm for the prospect. He wrote to a friend that he 'would probably have all the trouble, plague, responsibility and odium of new modelling the Government of New South Wales and restoring order and tranquillity there'. Re-modelling would certainly be needed, for over the two years since the comic-opera proceedings of January 26th, 1808, Botany Bay—as the English persisted in calling the colony—had had no settled Government.

When Macquarie's ship, the *Dromedary*, arrived at Rio de Janeiro, it was with some relief that he heard the news that John Macarthur and George Johnston had just passed through the port on their journey home. He bore with him Instructions to send Johnston home in close arrest. Over his fellow rebel, said to be the instigator of the whole affair, the military courts had no jurisdiction, but a worse fate had been planned for him—to be tried for High Treason before the Criminal Court of New South Wales, a trial which could have only one outcome. Colonel Macquarie must have given thanks to Providence for delivering him from beginning his reign with such an unpleasant task.

To the upright Macquarie, whose life had been passed in an atmosphere of unhesitating loyalty and devotion to duty, there could be no question how to regard a usurper of the power of the King's representative and his companion in mutiny.

The Colonel was a tall, good-looking man of courteous manners. Undoubtedly he had always been careful of the soldiers under his command; but the lower orders, especially those so debased as to become felons, were creatures with whose fate members of his society of rank and privilege had no concern. Yet at some time during that long voyage with his wife and newly appointed staff, a change in his mental attitude must have taken place. Perhaps as he read and re-read his Instructions, the notion crept into his mind that the colony over which he was going to rule did not only contain convicts under sentence and their gaolers, but also time-expired men who had begun a new life as free citizens, working to support themselves as best they could. Whether this new realisation came gradually or as sudden insight, from it grew that sympathy for the underdog on which the whole of his administration was built, and which in the end was to destroy him.

Like all new arrivals at Sydney, the Macquaries gazed around in enchantment as they sailed up the harbour, a delight which gave way to disillusion at the squalor of the town. Those—not many now—who could remember its early beginnings might marvel at the progress that had been made, but to the eyes of its new ruler it was just a mess. Though over recent years some comfortable homes had been erected on private property, the public buildings were in a dreadful state of dilapidation. The town had grown up haphazardly from the original tracks made for expediency in the reign of Governor Phillip. Macquarie, a man of orderly mind, looked at the lurching, unpaved roads, the mouldering houses, the ragged inhabitants, and shuddered.

These inhabitants, now threatened by another famine after some dry months, stared back at the dignified elderly gentleman in his smart, slim uniform, surrounded by his glittering staff. They had known so many Governors that the arrival of one more was just routine to the apathetic, rather pessimistic citizens. However, they liked the look of him and were glad of a pretext to light a bonfire or two that New Year's Eve. The ships let off some rockets, the band played, and everyone looked forward to a day off to celebrate the inauguration on January 1st, 1810.

The British Government had been firm in its intention not to allow the overthrow of a King's Representative to go on record. Macquarie had brought instructions from Lord Castlereagh addressed to 'Governor Bligh', directing that 'the day after you are liberated from arrest you are to receive Colonel Macquarie as your successor at Government House . . . and you will swear him into office'.

Bligh, however, had gone off to Van Diemen's Land in the *Porpoise*. Two weeks later he arrived 'pained and surprised' to find that the ceremony had taken place successfully without him.

The citizens of Sydney had also been surprised, even astonished, when after the normal business of inauguration, the reading of the Commission, the National Anthem and the Royal Salutes, their new ruler had stepped forward to address them as 'fellow-citizens and fellow-soldiers', asking for their support in the exercise of his new authority. Jaws fell open in cynical amazement at his hope that 'all the dissensions and jealousies which have unfortunately existed in the colony for some time will now terminate for ever'. He touched on the desirability of attending divine worship, of treating the native population with kindness and attention, and on the virtue of sobriety and discipline. But it was his closing words that really made them prick up their ears.

'I can assure you,' said Macquarie, 'that it will be the fault of the inhabitants themselves if they fail to be as comfortable and happy as any other of His Majesty's subjects. To make them so, as far as depends on myself, will not only be my duty, but at all times my chief happiness. The honest, sober and industrious inhabitant, whether free settler or convict, will ever find in me a friend and protector.'

The Macquarie era began like a rushing wind, swirling through dust and lumber, clearing out the corners and leaving the populace shaken up and breathless. The Governor kept strict office hours—land grants on Mondays, a levee for the gentlemen on Tuesdays: every morning had its allotted task. Fortunately, a store ship full of grain had come in shortly after his arrival to ward off the dreaded famine. The people were dazed. Nothing like this had ever happened before, but they recognised Macquarie's humanity and good intentions, and something almost like a community spirit dimly began to show.

Two weeks after the inauguration, Bligh arrived, all set for vengeance, but the new Governor had no desire to get involved in old quarrels. As far as he was concerned, the Rum Rebellion was a closed chapter. All he wished was that Bligh would now go home, but this the old sailor still refused to do. He took a cottage and hung about the colony, demanding viceregal honours. He made a trip to the Hawkesbury to visit those whom he still called his loyal supporters. Not for several months did he go on board the *Porpoise*, but even then he showed no signs of returning home till a personal blow really knocked him out at last. He had delayed his departure too long. The Commanding Officer of the newly arrived 73rd Regiment had fallen in love with the beautiful, now widowed, Mary

Putland; after a whirlwind courtship Bligh's daughter, who had staunchly stood by her father in his troubles, announced that she was staying in the colony to marry Colonel O'Connell. Captain Bligh might bluster, swear, and forbid the banns, but unhappily he was obliged to 'give the bride away' at the wedding reception at Government House, with the Governor and Mrs. Macquarie acting as hosts. Yet, he might finally have sailed off with a lighter heart had he realised that he had left behind in the new Second Lady an implacable enemy of his successor at Government House.

In recent years there has been a tendency among historians to build up Bligh as a much-wronged man with a heart of gold behind all his bluster. However, Macquarie, who certainly had no axe to grind, wrote at this time that he found the Commodore 'uncommonly harsh, and tyrannical in the extreme . . . a very improper person to be employed in any situation of trust or command . . . very generally detested by high, low, rich and poor'.

The departure of Bligh and the witnesses he took with him left the colony in a curious position. Eighteen months earlier, more than half the persons who had held any kind of authority had sailed home on a skin-saving expedition. Now, virtually everyone else connected with the old era had gone. Macquarie, looking round for men able and willing to take responsibility, did the only thing possible and appointed some of the most deserving of the emancipated convicts.

Before setting out for the colony, he had thought of it simply as a prison. One of his first surprises had been to find many of the prisoners—the Scots, the Irish, and the disciples of Tom Paine—not only unashamed, but glorying in their martyrdom.

Another surprise had been that the convicts—who were, after all, the great majority of the population—were taken for granted as they went about their business. True, they were liable to severe punishment for any misdemeanour, but even this was largely governed by the luck of the draw, or whether a prisoner had a mean and cruel employer or a fair one. While a large number were vicious characters in permanent trouble, a man prepared to work hard and mind his tongue could be a great deal better off than his opposite number in England. When such a man had served his time or obtained a pardon by good behaviour, he could take up land or go into business, hoping to be one day like Simeon Lord, whose white mansion adjoined the grounds of Government House; the 'crime' which had brought his seven years' transportation was the theft of some cotton stuff worth about 4/-; now his factories and stores were known all over the South Seas, and his ships sailed with the whaling fleet.

Only one survivor of the old days had not left the country—D'Arcy Wentworth.

Dr. Wentworth, who had never been a great one for colonial society, soon became a mainstay of the Macquarie régime. From Principal Surgeon he speedily became Chief Police Magistrate, Superintendent of Police, Hospital Contractor and Treasurer of the Police Fund. The witty Irishman, no frequenter of houses of the local squires, was always a welcome guest at the Governor's table, and his work received warm commendation in viceregal despatches to Lord Castlereagh.

One of the happiest achievements of that year was the holding of Australia's first race-meeting in Hyde Park, which all Sydney celebrated. Dr. Wentworth entered his horse, Gig; William Charles Wentworth was the rider and won in a canter.

Young Wentworth had begun to make his mark. He was one of the first freeborn sons of the colony, and there was no one who had not heard his name. Newly arrived from England, with his father in high favour at Government House, he already felt that a great future lay before him, even if its outline was still vague. He had been granted a property on the Nepean River, which he named Vermont. There he dabbled in geology and botany, picked up some native folk-lore and wrote a great deal of flamboyant verse, expounding his ideas to anyone who would listen. In a colony not given to introspective thought, he was something of an oddity—what today might be termed an intellectual; but he was certainly no pale dreamer. It could not have been only to please his father that Macquarie, whose Provost Marshall had gone to England in Bligh's retinue, appointed William Wentworth to that rank—the first native-born son to be appointed to a senior official position. The duties resembled those of a sheriff, and it must have been curious to see such a very young gentleman presiding at meetings of grizzled citizens more than twice his age, but we may be sure that Acting Provost Marshall Wentworth himself was not abashed.

D'Arcy Junior, his brother, was also favoured by the Governor, through whose influence the boy also achieved a 'first'—the first native Australian to receive a commission in the British army, in which he served with distinction. The third brother entered the Navy, but unfortunately was drowned while still a midshipman.

New Year's Day was always an occasion for speeches, of back-patting for past achievements, and of allusions to what the colonists considered ought to be done in the year to come. At the celebrations of 1812, a new note crept into William Wentworth's speech, a tendril feeling out towards what was to become his life's work, the idea that one day the colony would be able to govern itself on the lines of the British Constitution.

After a wonderful first year in which everything seemed to go right, Macquarie was beginning to find himself beset with troubles. With no one to tell him in advance, he had had to feel out by experience the extraordinary social set-up of the colony of New South Wales, a society unique in the world then and ever after.

This society was divided into horizontal layers. At the base of the pyramid was the reason for its existence—the convicts under sentence, creatures with no rights beyond their meagre food. Superior to them were the emancipists and the poor free settlers. Above this level came a class whose members considered themselves to be a completely different species of humanity, the so-called Exclusives, comprising the rich free settlers and the officers, military and civil. The apex of the structure, the absolute authority, was the Governor, representing the King himself.

However, the layers of this pyramid-cake were not rigidly separated, but mixed up in a very confusing fashion. An Exclusive would do business with an emancipist, while refusing to meet him on friendly terms. Struggling free settlers mixed socially with poor emancipists, but looked down on them; they even secretly despised the *rich* emancipists who, secure in their wealth, had no time for the poor free farmer battling to feed his family from his precarious crops.

So when on St. Patrick's Day His Excellency gave a dinner to some sixty convicts employed around Government House, the Exclusives were outraged, and his continued friendliness with the loyal emancipists to whom he had entrusted power and responsibility brought down on his head the wrath even of the officers of his own regiment, who had not taken long to become soaked in local prejudice.

Not only social prejudices wrinkled the Governor's brow. He had been ordered to construct roads and bridges, to effect some of the improvements which, heaven knew, were crying out to be done. With zest and energy he plunged into an elaborate building programme, informing the authorities at home that this would cost money. Even before his letters could arrive he was deluged with angry despatches urging economy. Why was the colony costing so much more now than it did in the time of Governor King? demanded the Colonial Office.

There were a great many reasons why, hundreds of them in the shape of new convicts who continued to arrive in ever-growing numbers—not to mention the new settlers, who often arrived from England armed with grants of land, issued to them by influential men at home who had not the slightest idea of conditions in New South Wales.

As the population increased, the continual cry went up for more land from rich settlers like the Blaxland Brothers, whose herds of cattle were outgrowing their pastures on the Nepean River. When in 1813 Gregory Blaxland approached Governor Macquarie with a plan for getting across the Blue Mountains, he was received with considerable attention, the more so as another great drought was threatening the settlers with a new famine.

For twenty-five years this awe-inspiring range had allured men and thrown them back defeated, caging them into the thirty-five or so miles of thickly wooded country between the mountains and the sea. Governor Phillip himself had been one of them, and the intrepid George Bass had taken time off from exploration by sea to attack the mountains with ropes and grappling irons; the Frenchman Barrallier had tried his luck, and so had Cayley, the temperamental botanist sent out by Sir Joseph Banks. After this, Governor King wrote to Banks: 'The crossing of the mountains must be given up, as the rocks to the west are the most barren and forbidding which man, animals and birds have ever been strangers to.'

But now Blaxland, after two excursions, had a theory as to how the mountains might be overcome. Before approaching the Governor he worked out his plan with his young neighbour on the Nepean River.

'I'll come with you,' William Wentworth said at once.

The third member of the party that set out on May 11th, 1813, with four convict servants and twenty-four horses, was Lieutenant William Lawson, an experienced surveyor. It was a tough climb. Sometimes they could not advance more than two miles a day, but on they struggled, always avoiding the gullies and clinging to the actual ridge-top, for that was the secret of Blaxland's plan. The trouble had always been not so much the height of these ranges, but the chaotic way in which the lofty sandstone plateau was split by sheer precipices and ravines. A climber might manage to push through dense timber along a spur to find himself on the brink of a gorge looking straight down on to tree-tops far below; or, if by superhuman efforts he descended into the valley which seemed to wind between the perpendicular slopes, before long the way would be blocked by yet another unscaleable precipice.

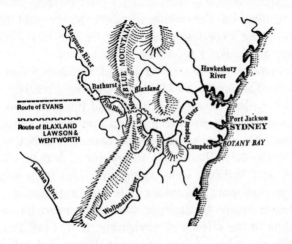

The route followed by Blaxland, Lawson, and Wentworth was wild and rugged, but after fifteen days of hard endeavour they reached a point where the hoped-for view burst on their eyes—mile after mile of green, well watered country; 'sufficient', wrote Blaxland, 'to support the stock of this colony for thirty years'.

The three explorers had not crossed the main range, but they had seen what lay beyond—fine, watered pasture extending as far as their eyes could see. It was the most important discovery yet made, so important that the Governor for the time being did nothing about it!

'I *dare* not!' he told Mrs. Macquarie, the one person with whom he could discuss his problems. 'If those who are crying out for land knew what lies beyond the mountains . . .' In his mind he saw a stampede, a grabbing free-for-all, bushrangers striving with escaped convicts, aborigines driven still further from their hunting grounds and turning on the white invaders. So he said little, but sent the experienced surveyor George Evans to go further and make a report on what he found.

Wentworth did not come out of this expedition unscathed. The weeks of climbing, soaking, freezing, and exhaustion had affected his lungs, and his father thought that a sea trip might cure his persistent cough. Garnham Blaxcell, Macarthur's business partner, was about to set off for the Friendly Islands to try for a deal in sandalwood, and William went along with him on a voyage that proved more hazardous than was anticipated.

Always ready to attempt something new, he began dabbling in the science of navigation. It was exhilarating to take the wheel as the schooner dipped and rolled in the deep-blue water, but the Pacific held its dangers, as the strangers discovered when they braved a hitherto unknown shore. On one of the Cook Islands, the landing party was suddenly attacked by wild-eyed savages with bared teeth and menacing spears. These were no gentle Australians to be won over by trumpery gifts of beads and looking-glasses. Hastily the white men retreated, except for the leading sailor who was surrounded and clubbed to his knees. It seemed his end had come when one of the savage attackers clapped a hand to his shoulder and stared in alarm in the direction from which he had heard a sharp crack. At the sight of the strange object in Wentworth's hand, smoke still rising from its end, the whole frizzy-haired gang fell back before the white man's magic.

'Lucky you had your pistol ready,' said Blaxcell, 'or we might all be suffering the fate of Captain Cook. What a loss that was to the world!' Everyone in New South Wales knew the story of Cook's last ill-fated voyage in the *Resolution*. Young Bligh had been in the ship's company, so had the soon-to-be-famous explorer Vancouver. Landing at Owhyhi (Hawaii), Cook had been held under water and butchered. The rescue party, arriving three days later, could only recover his head, hands and a few charred bones, which grisly relics were buried at sea.

To the mind of William Charles Wentworth, the world had just narrowly escaped another such loss. More and more he was certain that he had been born a Man of Destiny, the first of his country's sons who would be pre-eminent in whatever calling he finally decided to follow. He certainly had one advantage—his powers were never handicapped by false modesty.

D'Arcy Wentworth's hope that his son would become a surgeon was doomed by William's undeniable squint. However skilled a diagnosis, however deft the hand holding the scalpel, prospective patients might well be discouraged by a doctor one of whose eyes appeared to be gazing over their shoulder. At that time there were not so many professions open to the sons of gentlemen. As second choice, his father favoured the army, but William himself was drawn towards the law. In any case he was to go to England again before entering any profession, and for the time being he was in no hurry to leave. Too many interesting things were going on in Sydney.

Colonel Macquarie was unquestionably an autocrat, though a benevolent one. He would admit no challenge to his supremacy; in consequence, he found himself in conflict with several men who were accustomed to having their own way. Chief among these was the Reverend Samuel Marsden, known as 'the flogging parson', whose stocky, bucolic figure, usually armed with a horsewhip, was hated and feared for the brutal sentences of hundreds of lashes which he imposed from the magisterial bench. He was a better farmer than healer of souls, rivalling John Macarthur himself as a producer of fine wool. Marsden had just returned from England, where he had hobnobbed with such men as the Archbishop of Canterbury and William Wilberforce, gaining a high reputation for his zeal in spreading the gospel in the Pacific Islands. He was furious to find himself appointed to serve on the board of the new turnpike road along with two ex-convict magistrates, Simeon Lord and Andrew Thompson. He immediately sent off to London venomous reports of Macquarie's mismanagement, and from then on set about undermining the Governor's reputation.

Another headache for the Governor was caused by quarrels with his legal advisers. Judge Advocate Ellis Bent and his brother Jeffrey, the Supreme Court Judge, joined the number of those who were busily writing home to criticise the Governor's every action. So ardently did they intrigue against him that Macquarie was driven to warning the Home authorities that if they were not removed, he would himself resign. The Secretary of State acted by recalling Jeffrey Bent, and almost at the same time his brother very conveniently died. Ellis Bent's successor as Judge Advocate, Mr. John Wylde, was something new to the colony—a man who was experienced in the law and without the desire to enrich himself either by graft or by profiteering in trade.

The London court-martial of Major Johnston for mutiny against Governor Bligh had inevitably ended in that officer being cashiered from the army. However, since he was still under the patronage of the Duke of Northumberland, this did him little harm. He returned to New South Wales in high good humour, prepared to pass his remaining years on his Nepean estate in convivial retirement.

The case of John Macarthur presented greater difficulty, for he could not be tried by a military court, nor by a Criminal Court in England. The evidence at the trial had convinced the authorities that he was the instigator and mainspring of the Rum Rebellion, and they had no intention of letting him loose to sow more disaffection. As far as the law was concerned, he was free to go home; but the instruction to Macquarie to have him tried in Sydney had never been cancelled. Macarthur knew well that if he set foot in New South Wales he would soon be labouring in a chain gang, even if he escaped the gallows. So he stayed on in London, fuming and frustrated, writing directions by every mail to Elizabeth on the care of his property. From afar he intrigued and interfered in everything that concerned the running of the colony. At first he had approved of Macquarie's appointment, but when news reached him of the Viceroy's policy of friendship with the emancipists, the violence of his disgust almost scorched the paper of the letters he sent to New South Wales.

The Governor's friendliness towards the emancipists caused growing resentment. The 73rd Regiment was replaced by the 46th, whose officers had sworn in advance to have no social intercourse with anyone who had come to the colony against his will; on one occasion, a body of them left the Governor's table rather than sit with such a man.

Soon a first-class row blew up over the circulation of a particularly scurrilous 'pipe', a satirical doggerel mocking their Commanding Officer, Colonel Molle. For months, scandal and accusations rocked Sydney till, when a scapegoat was about to be put on trial, D'Arcy Wentworth revealed that his son William had written the verses before sailing for England early in 1816. Young Wentworth, though considering himself an exclusive by birth —one of the 'pure merinos', as they were called—had been strongly in favour of Macquarie's policy of giving responsibility to emancipists worthy to hold it.

Part of the disgust he felt for Macquarie's opponents, whom he described as being 'more cruel than vultures', came from their treatment of Dr. Redfern, his father's chief assistant and a favoured friend of the Governor.

William Redfern had been transported for life (on reprieve from the death sentence) at the age of nineteen for having in effect said 'Go it, boys!' during the mutiny at the Nore, when the seamen rose in protest against their shocking living conditions. The lad, then a surgeon's

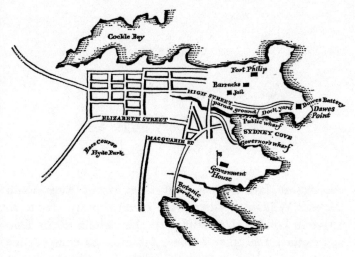

Sydney in 1821

mate, had done so well as to be granted a Surgeon's Commission in New South Wales, but to the Exclusives, though they might allow him to save their lives when they fell sick, Dr. Redfern was still a pariah.

CHAPTER IX

A SHATTERING
DISCOVERY

HAVING at last torn himself away from New South Wales, William Wentworth could hardly wait to arrive in London. Unfortunately, the captain of the *Emu* had exactly the opposite idea, and after an exasperating dawdle across the Indian Ocean, the traveller landed at Cape Town and transferred himself bag and baggage to a French ship, the *Révolutionnaire*—a name bodeful for his future.

His plans for the next few years were not yet precise. That he would study the law was certain, but in the far-off colony it had been difficult to be sure how best to set about it. However, his family had a powerful patron in Lord Fitzwilliam, whom he proposed to approach in a befitting manner.

He also had personal friends in the Macarthur family, with whom he had been intimate in his boyhood days at Parramatta. In addition to the head of the family, all the young males were now in London. James and William, having completed their education, had been joined by military veteran Edward on the Continent, where their father had recently taken the boys on a tour of the vineyards. The party had returned loaded with plant cuttings with which to start a wine industry in New South Wales.

The second son, John junior, was only a short time away from becoming the first Australian to be called to the English Bar. For once Wentworth found himself second in such a race, but with the excuse that young John had been in England ever since his father had brought him over in 1801. With a brilliant brain and many desirable contacts, he was a friend for Wentworth to cultivate, and for a time the two young men were on fairly intimate terms.

Of all the Macarthur sons, this one above all had inherited his father's nature. The younger boys were 'moderns', but the two Johns shared the outlook of the eighteenth-century magnate. To them, society was a divinely appointed state in which it was given to the exalted few to own the land and possess unquestioned right to service.

'God bless the Squire and his relations,
And keep us in our proper stations'—
that was the becoming attitude for the lower classes. Nothing could exceed the fury of the die-hard Whig for the new rascally 'democrats' who were trying to give the rabble ideas that Jack, if not yet as good as his master, was at least entitled to earn enough wages to keep his family in crusts.

The Macarthurs longed for news from home. Tales of Macquarie's Sydney and memories of happy days at Parramatta were exchanged for advice, spiced with much grumbling from the irascible magnate, who had now become a victim of the rheumatic gout which was to plague him for the rest of his life.

At that time, Wentworth cherished the idea of paying court to Elizabeth Macarthur; though whether the attraction was from the heart or with an eye to the advantage of becoming her father's son-in-law, no one can say. The exalted opinion he held of his own powers must have proved irritating to those not gifted with his self-assurance. He squinted, he was an untidy dresser, heavy-shouldered and clumsy in his carriage, but the force of his personality was such as to overshadow disabilities which became even less of a handicap as he approached maturity and fame. However, nothing came of his courtship of Elizabeth Macarthur, and he applied himself to his study of the law.

Five years of work lay ahead before he could be called to the Bar, and even a 'pure merino' needed influence to get into Chambers at the Inns of Court. William, therefore, addressed a letter to his father's patron, setting forth his qualifications—not as yet great—and his hopes, for which the sky was the limit.

'In selecting the profession of the Law,' he wrote, 'I calculate upon acquainting myself with all the excellence of the British Constitution, and hope at some future period to advocate successfully the right of my country to participate in its advantages. This is the point to which my chief efforts shall be directed.' He also stressed that he was a collateral descendant of Charles I's Minister, the famous Thomas Wentworth, Earl of Strafford.

For his own reasons, Lord Fitzwilliam secured the young man's entry into the Inner Temple, where he settled down to five years' study not only of the law, but of politics. Attending debates in the House of Commons and —following his childhood habit—listening to the conversations of people in all walks of life, he soon realised that he had a front seat at one of the most stimulating periods in the advance of Britain to become the world's leading power.

The year 1815 had been a turning point in history. After it, nothing was ever quite the same again. Every country in Europe was exhausted, but in England the changes were more pronounced than anywhere else; for, from being an agricultural country, Britain was advancing into the Industrial Revolution.

Perhaps the Government could be forgiven for not understanding what was going on, for nothing like it had ever happened before. There had always been difficulties at the end of a war, when the men came home to pick up the threads of their lives again by tilling the neglected land or by working at their old handicrafts and trades. But now there were neither foreign trade nor government orders; for such private orders as did exist, the products of the cottage craftsman were giving place to the cheaper goods produced in factories by the dreaded machinery.

To make matters worse, the landowners—some of them the fathers of the land-grabbers of New South Wales—had begun to enclose the common land that had always belonged to the people. Parliament allowed this, for large farms with money spent on them were more productive than smallholdings, but it spelt death for the yeoman farmers who had been the pride of England. They either had to work for the new owners, or go into factories, in either case at a starvation wage. Factory work meant that the workers must leave the farms and the villages for the towns; so their food had to be transported to the

E

towns, the raw material must be brought there and the finished goods taken away. All this meant new roads and canals, and eventually railways: a complete upheaval of the former way of living, and all of it happening over a short period.

The new conditions were going to be fine for the rich, but to the poor they brought misery and starvation. Desperate rioters smashed the machinery, and were hanged or transported for it. The new Corn Laws had sent unemployment soaring; workless men, marching in procession, were arrested. When a crowd set off 'to capture the Tower of London', that project so reminiscent of the French Revolution sent the rulers of Britain into a perfect frenzy of fear.

Caught up in these stirring events, Wentworth's brain was in constant ferment. He went to Paris for a while, for relaxation and to enlarge his knowledge of the world. At the age of twenty-six, he felt able to view his future with great complacency. His father was a rich and respected figure, owner of many thousand acres; he himself was already a landed proprietor in his own right. In due time he would marry a suitable wife, who would give him sons to follow in the possession of vast estates, founding an honourable dynasty which would wield great power over the development of his native land. He returned to London refreshed, to take up his studies with his accustomed energy, when out of the blue came the stroke which rocked his whole conception of life to its foundations.

It seems almost incredible that William Wentworth had passed his twenty-sixth birthday without hearing the story that was common knowledge to every Exclusive and convict in New South Wales, but which burst upon him without any warning; but it must be remembered that he had first left Sydney as a young boy, returning after his school days to find his father high in the Governor's favour and holding so many posts of honour that it was quite hard to remember them all.

So there is no need to explain his shock when, while occupied with some research in connection with early colonisation, he came upon a public letter addressed to Lord Sidmouth by the Honourable Henry Grey Bennet, M.P., in which he read the astounding statement that his father D'Arcy Wentworth had been transported to New South Wales in 1789 as a convict! The statement was made as a matter of course, not of conjecture, and was followed by various detrimental remarks on the character of the presumed felon.

The son's first reaction was one of towering rage at such a libel. He at once sought an interview with Mr. Bennet, who received him coolly, with no sign of repentance. Perhaps, he admitted, the letter had been a little carelessly worded, but the fact remained that D'Arcy Wentworth had as a young medical student in fact been arrested for highway robbery and tried at the Old Bailey. True, he had been acquitted, but only because no witness had come forward to identify him. The member of Parliament insinuated that the young Irishman had escaped sentence only because influential friends had persuaded him to take himself off to New South Wales as soon as possible, and stay there. Although not 'convicted' in the strictly legal sense, D'Arcy Wentworth was to all intents and purposes a convict, regarded and treated as such.

This rude awakening from his vision of himself as a—almost as *the*—First Exclusive of Australia by right of birth, dealt William Wentworth a wound which took years to heal, if heal it ever did. His whole outlook on life was shattered. Gone was the subconscious feeling that his championship of Macquarie's policy of fair play for emancipists was a noble gesture on the part of a 'pure merino'. Even if his beloved and respected father had never worn leg-irons, he knew now that his mother, too, had been a convict, a young Staffordshire woman, sentenced to transportation for some minor offence. D'Arcy had met her on board that accursed convict ship *Neptune*, and continued to live with her on Norfolk Island.

Research in the public press found his father, then 'a tall, handsome and burly young medical student', referred to as 'the notorious highwayman', though the assertion that he was only acquitted on condition he went to Botany Bay was not true, according to Lord Fitzwilliam, who testified that he sailed freely and of his own volition.

His noble kinsman had always felt a slight responsibility over the unfortunate affair. When D'Arcy Wentworth, son of a Portadown innkeeper of the same name, came to London from Ireland as a young man and contrived to get himself introduced to Lord Fitzwilliam, the latter was so struck by his charm and exceptional good looks that he took considerable notice of him. This patronage led to the youth getting into company and habits beyond his means, to gambling debts and, in despair, to highway robbery. D'Arcy was too remarkable a figure—or too little adept at highwaymanship—to escape detection, and it was only his patron's intervention that led to his being given the chance of emigrating as a free man.

THE LONDON
CONVICT MAID.

Charlotte W——, the subject of this narrative, is a native of London, born of honest parents, she was early taught the value and importance of honesty and virtue; but unhapily ere her attaining the age of maturity, her youthful affections were placed on a young Tradesman, and to raise money to marry her lover, she yielded to the temptation to rob her master, and his property being found in her possession, she was immediately apprehended, tried at the Old Bailey Sessions, convicted, and sentenced to seven years transportation. On her arrival at Hobart Town, she sent her mother a very affecting and pathetic letter, from which the following verses have been composed, and they are here published by particular desire, in the confident hope that this account of her sufferings will serve as an example to deter other females from similar practices.

YE London maids attend to me,
While I relate my misery,
Thro' London Streets I oft have stray'd,
But now I am a Convict Maid.

In innocence I once did live,
In all the joy that peace could give,
But sin my youthful heart betrayed,
And now I am a Convict Maid.

To wed my lover I did try,
To take my master's property,
So all my guilt was soon displayed,
And I became a Convict Maid.

Then I was soon to prison sent,
To wait in fear my punishment,
When at the bar I stood dismayed,
Since doomed to be a Convict Maid.

At length the Judge did me address,
Which filled with pain my aching breast
To Botany Bay you will be conveyed,
For seven years a Convict Maid.

For seven years oh, how I sighed,
While my poor mother loudly cried,
My lover wept, and thus he said,
May God be with my Convict Maid.

To you that hear my mournful tale,
I cannot half my grief reveal,
No sorrow yet has been pourtrayed,
Like that of the poor Convict Maid

Far from my friends and home so dear,
My punishment is most severe,
My woe is great and I'm afraid,
That I shall die a Convict Maid.

I toil each day in grief and pain,
And sleepless through the night remain,
My constant toils are unrepaid,
And wretched is the Convict Maid.

Oh could I but once more be free,
I'd ne'er again a captive be,
But I would seek some honest trade,
And ne'er become a Convict Maid.

BIRT, Printer, 39, Great St. Andrew Street, Seven Dials.

Ballads like these were sung in the streets of London, and their texts sold as broadsheets

Before this knowledge compelled him to accept the truth, William Wentworth had written to his father: 'Deeply as I am mortified to find there is the smallest shadow of foundation for the circulation of any report prejudicial to your reputation, cut as I am to the quick . . . still you may rest assured that I will compel this lying slanderer to make you the most public and complete reparation for so infamous a calumny, or else spill the last drop of my heart's blood in the effort.'

But it was no use. Bennet did make some sort of apology, but it would do no good to pursue the matter. In London nobody cared, and in New South Wales people would only laugh. The story had been public property there for twenty-six years. That was why, the son reasoned now, D'Arcy had avoided Society—to prevent Society avoiding *him*. Though an officer now resident in Sydney had actually been present at the Old Bailey when the charge of robbery under arms was dismissed, the slur had persisted, and in the Bigge Report, shortly to appear, Wentworth senior was still referred to as an ex-convict.

So now William had to patch up his wounded pride, and approach public life from a new angle. His vision of himself as Australia's First Citizen still remained. Several years had yet to pass before he could qualify as a barrister, and after that he planned to take his degree at Cambridge. If he could no longer meet the arrogant members of aristocratic society on equal terms, his pen must be his weapon. He began to write a book meant to bring the potential importance of Australia home to the general public in Britain, which still looked upon

'Botany Bay' as a savage barren land, fit only for convicts.

In New South Wales, the struggle between Governor and Exclusives was becoming ever more acute, though under Macquarie the colony was more comfortable and better run than ever before. The convict architect Francis Greenway was transforming Sydney with his graceful sandstone buildings. The Governor's pride and joy—the Bank of New South Wales—had been inaugurated, and at last the colony had its own currency: the silver 'holey dollar', worth 5s., with the circle punched out of that hole forming 'the dump', worth 1s. 3d.

But Macquarie's enemies, led by the Reverend Samuel Marsden, were hounding him to destruction. An injudicious court-martial of the clergyman Benjamin Vale for flouting viceregal authority was the pretext for a petition against the Governor to be sent to London. Wentworth, whose name had already begun to be recognised as one to be reckoned with in matters concerning Australia, made strenuous efforts to prevent this petition from being presented.

Much of the tight-fisted policy which had kept successive Governors so short of money had been caused by the needs of the war with Napoleon, though apart from that, every Minister in turn had firmly held that the British taxpayer should not be squeezed to 'provide luxuries for a receptacle for convicts'. But now the 'Colony of Disgracefuls' had taken on a new look. Tidings of the new road, constructed by William Cox to lead over the Blue Mountains to the fertile land beyond, caused a rush of applications for passages to Australia. Governor Macquarie received instructions to push on with explorations along the rivers which, it was thought, must exist to water the interior of what was now known to be a great continent.

In England itself, life for the poor was becoming a savage struggle. Certainly people were free—free to starve, for there was little work and wages were not enough to live on. Unrest and lawlessness increased, and now the people's leaders began to work for reform inside parliament itself. One day in August, 1819, it was announced that a famous agitator called 'Orator Hunt' would address a meeting in St. Peter's Fields in Manchester in favour of parliamentary reform; when a crowd of fifty thousand assembled, the authorities lost their heads, and though there was no disorder, the Yeomanry were ordered to disperse the people. Up rode the soldiers brandishing their swords, but such a vast concourse could not be melted away by shouting commands. As the people milled to and fro, the mounted soldiers charged the mob.

The result was carnage. Eleven people, including two women and a child, were killed. Hundreds more fell, to be trampled on by their friends, for once down, no one could rise—and all this only four years after England's soldiers had fought at Waterloo to save her liberty!

'Peterloo', the name people gave in acid mockery to the massacre of Manchester, became a war-cry in the long fight of the British working-class movement.

Following closely on Peterloo, spurred on by the ruthless Lord Castlereagh, Parliament passed the six 'Gag Acts'; in England it could now be a felony to meet together, to air grievances, to combine for protection. Starving workers told one another that even the convicts in New South Wales were better off; for to these people, weak with hunger and almost without hope, tales had trickled through of the good conditions now enjoyed by ex-convicts in 'Botany Bay'. The legends of flogging and famine were forgotten; even the convict ships now had been robbed of their terrors. Suddenly there was a rush to commit 'crimes' that would bring sentences of transportation, and men and women standing in line to board vessels for New South Wales sang cheerfully at the prospect of free foreign travel to His Majesty's colony in the South Seas.

To those in power, the trend was very unsettling. It was as though their guns had recoiled upon them, injuring the shooter instead of the enemy. Reports showed that Governor Macquarie, not satisfied with exalting emancipists above their betters, was engaged in a building programme of hospitals, public edifices and palaces quite unsuitable for the penal settlement the place was supposed to be.

> The rich man in his castle, the poor man at his gate,
> God made them high and lowly, and ordered their estate.

That was the hymn which the people in power sang on Sundays, and thoroughly believed in. God had certainly never intended the prisoner to enjoy his punishment, and if transported convicts embraced their chains, then conditions in New South Wales would have to be the subject of a serious enquiry.

On the other hand, the discovery of fine pasture land put a new face on the problem. Now that the Industrial Revolution was covering Britain with towns and factories, there would soon not be enough agricultural land left for the farmers to grow food.

Suppose the colony were to be thrown open to free

settlers, with perhaps some financial aid to induce them to emigrate? It would be easy enough to establish new convict stations where felons could be made to suffer for their crimes in a proper manner, instead of being mollycoddled, as was apparently the case now.

Accordingly, it was decided that a London barrister named Bigge, the kinsman of an Under-Secretary of State, should go out armed with powers to make a full report on everything connected with the way in which the colony was being run. In the year of Peterloo, Mr. Bigge set out upon his mission.

CHAPTER X

SOWING THE SEED

Up to the year 1816, no person having the idea of settling could enter New South Wales without leave of the Governor. But as conditions in Britain worsened, the more emigrants who betook themselves overseas the better, and all restrictions were therefore removed. Now, every ship brought more free settlers, and before Governor Macquarie left in 1822, the population had risen to nearly 40,000 persons.

Part of this increase was directly due to William Charles Wentworth.

With his private world shaken in its foundations, he had to reshape his whole way of thinking. Life had been planned on the assumption that he would always be a natural leader of aristocratic society. That dream was dead. A leader—yes, he would be that, but by his own talents, not by right of birth. Even though in years to come his achievements might wipe out the memory of the past, he himself would never be quite certain that it had been forgotten, not momentarily overlooked.

Actually, his outlook had been changing ever since his arrival in England: the challenge of the infant democracy struggling into life had drawn him into sympathy with the reformers. To a writer of flamboyant verse, what could appeal more strongly than the words of Shelley and Byron, those brilliant young poets who were both ardent supporters of the new trend. Had not Byron in the House of Lords demanded 'mercy for these men meagre with famine and sullen with despair'? Law studies occupied only part of Wentworth's time. As well as taking in knowledge, he needed to pour out, to release the flood of energy that possessed him. Above everything, he longed to advance the interests of his native land, and soon he was launching the first campaign in history to attract British migrants to Australia—a campaign which, after nearly a century and a half, is still going strong.

The year 1819 had seen the publication of a volume by William Wentworth entitled: *A Statistical, Historical and Political Description of the Colony of New South Wales and its Dependent Settlements in Van Diemen's Land, With a Particular Enumeration of the Advantages which these Colonies offer for Emigration, and their Superiority in many respects over those possessed by the United States of America.*

This book caused a considerable sensation. With it, he captured another record; it was the first book to be published by a native Australian, and he could scarcely have done his country a greater service at that time. In the desperate aftermath of the French War, a great tide of human beings was pouring out of Europe, to the Cape Colony and to the 'promised land' in North America. The thought of Australia—the name was at last catching on—as a country in which to begin a new life as a free settler had entered few heads until Wentworth put it there. Only those in high places had access to the reports of the vast new pastures discovered since the author of that book had himself helped to open the way over the Blue Mountains less than six years earlier. To the popular mind, Australia was still a barren wilderness inhabited solely by convicts and cannibals.

Here, then, was a voice proclaiming that no other country in the world offered such chances to the new settler. True, he would have to start from scratch, for the land was not equipped with everything the new arrival might require. But Wentworth's advice ran from the general to the particular. Members of various trades found lists of the articles they should take for their special crafts: nails, locks, sieves, sickles and saddles, pans and churns. Everything could be carried in sailing ships, and vessels were now available which could make the voyage in not much more than five months.

And hundreds did go. For some, the conditions proved too harsh, but others made good and laid a sound foundation for their children's children.

The book with its impressive title sold out and made a profit. New printings were demanded, and in the new edition readers got even more for their money. Wentworth's ideas were flowering, and with his presentation of a dream-country he was what we should today call its first propagandist.

Lieutenant Phillip Parker King, R.N., in the *Mermaid*, had completed Flinders's survey of the Australian coast, proving it to be one vast island continent. Wentworth, feeling no doubt that an advertiser should have complete knowledge of what he sells, approached Lord Bathurst at the Colonial Office, to whom he was by now no stranger. Recalling to his Lordship's memory his own exploits on the Blue Mountains, he requested permission to 'explore the continent from its eastern extremity to its western'.

Even the noble Lord, with no personal knowledge of the fierceness with which Australia met its would-be discoverers, was startled at such a comprehensive suggestion. Could he have been granted a vision of the agonised years to come of struggle by dedicated explorers to cross the burning wastes and trackless bush, the sunstroke and thirst, the abandoned skeletons of men and beasts, he could scarcely have been less encouraging. It was useless for Wentworth to declare, 'having been born in the colony, I feel an interest in all that concerns it that can only attach itself to a place of one's nativity'. Lord Bathurst had other plans, and urged the would-be explorer to go away and apply himself to his studies.

Deprived of a heroic physical outlet, Wentworth bent his energies to his country's internal reform, and here at last he embraced what was to become his life's work. The new edition of his book developed the theme on which he had touched previously. The more he studied English law and politics, the more convinced he became that one day Australia would govern herself as a free nation. Obviously such a dawning was still a long way off, and agreement by free will was just a rosy dream. In a colony as torn with feuds and jealousies as New South Wales had been ever since Arthur Phillip sailed away in 1792, it was hard to imagine any government not imposed by iron control from the top.

Sitting alone in his room, or on long walks into the country at Hampstead or Highgate Hill, he wrestled with his thoughts and new ideas. Had not the deplorable conditions in New South Wales come about because those who really ruled the country were men with the same principles—or lack of them—as those who from the beginning had seized power for their own enrichment? The Old Gang was still in control. John Macarthur had been permitted to return home by promising to keep out of politics, but behind the scenes the inveterate rebel was as active as ever, with his sons at hand to carry out his orders.

The Government emissary sent out to report on how the colony was run, Mr. J. R. Bigge, had fallen completely under Macarthur's influence. In his report, Governor Macquarie's encouragement of small homesteads owned by self-supporting farmers was condemned out of hand, as was his policy for the advancement of the emancipists. Such men as Dr. Redfern were the target of his sarcasm: 'The surgeon's manner,' he wrote, 'betrayed an entire forgetfulness in himself of that occurrence in his life which he will find difficult to erase from the memory of others'. In the righteous eyes of Mr. Bigge, twenty-three years of work in the public interest could not wipe out a boy's 'crime' of encouraging hungry sailors to strike for better rations.

It was natural that along with Dr. Redfern the even wealthier and more successful Dr. D'Arcy Wentworth, owner of 40,000 acres and holder of as many public offices as the famous Poo-Bah, should come under Mr. Bigge's lash. Once more William had the anguish of seeing his father branded as an ex-convict, and again the son sprang to defend his name. In a new edition of his *Description of the Colony* in 1824 he fulminated against the Bigge Report, indignantly defending not only his father, but the Governor himself.

For Macquarie, the official condemnation of the results for which he had striven over a longer term of office than any of his predecessors was the final straw. Three times he had begged to be released, and at last his plea was granted; the appointment of Sir Thomas Brisbane, long rumoured, was confirmed.

Macquarie's departure marked the end of an era. Though good manners and humanity disguised the fact, he had been as much of an autocrat as any of the naval Governors, but now the time for absolute rule had passed. Henceforth, the authority of the Viceroys would be subject to review by Whitehall, and in 1823 a Legislative Council was set up in New South Wales with power to make laws for the peace, welfare and good government of the colony, ' . . . always providing that such were not repugnant to the laws of England'. Wentworth had seen the Bill through the British Parliament, having himself had a hand in drafting some of its clauses.

'The dictatorial and menacing tone of this stripling Australian'—Robert Wardell, the barrister and close friend of Wentworth, ducked, and the cushion flung at his head flew past, to drop against the wall. 'But you should be *pleased*, William!' he protested, holding up the *Edinburgh Review* from which he had been reading. 'Better a condescending notice than none at all, and the *Review* doesn't deny that a Legislative Council would not have been set up in New South Wales if you hadn't goaded the Government past endurance.'

'Stripling, indeed!' snorted Wentworth. But that was the only word he was entitled to resent. It *had* needed menacing words to get the Bill through Parliament, even

THE OLD VICEROY

From the pen of our Favourite Laureate Bard,
Mr Robinson.

*And to be sung at the Colonial Anniversary Dinner,
26th of January, 1824.*

What care we for the skill to scan
  The bright stars overhead?
Give us for Governor the man
  Who rules and is obey'd.

CHORUS:

Macquarie was the prince of men!
  Australia's pride and Joy!
We ne'er shall see his like again;
  Here's to the OLD Viceroy!

OUR gallant Governor has gone,
  Across the rolling sea,
To tell the King on England's throne,
  What merry men are we.

CHORUS:

Macquarie was the prince of men!
  Australia's pride and Joy!
We ne'er shall see his like again;
  Here's to the OLD Viceroy!

Freeman and convict, man and boy,
  Are all agreed! I'll wager,
They'd sell their last slop shirt to buy
  A ticket for the Major.

CHORUS:

Macquarie was the prince of men!
  Australia's pride and Joy!
We ne'er shall see his like again;
  Here's to the OLD Viceroy!

Some Governors have heads, I think;
  But some have none at all:
Cheer up, my lads; push round the drink,
  And drown care in Bengal.

CHORUS:

Macquarie was the prince of men!
  Australia's pride and Joy!
We ne'er shall see his like again;
  Here's to the OLD Viceroy!

Here's to Sir Thomas's release,
  The old Viceroy's return;
And fourteen years beyond the seas
  For thee, Frederick Goulburn.

CHORUS:

Macquarie was the prince of men!
  Australia's pride and Joy!
We ne'er shall see his like again;
  Here's to the OLD Viceroy!

This tribute to the retiring Governor Macquarie was published in
the Australian newspaper *The Colonist*

a Bill so cut about and re-written that he could only describe the result as a crude amendment, a wretched mongrel of a substitute. The rights for the emancipists were still missing; so was a Supreme Court and full trial by jury, but it was a beginning, and the 'stripling Australian' had good cause for satisfaction.

He had taken his degree at Cambridge, about which he had cherished no doubts. Neither had he any doubts that he would win the Chancellor's medal with his poem 'Australasia', which described the crossing of the Blue Mountains:

'As the meteor shoots athwart the night
The boundless champaign burst upon our sight
Till, nearer seen, the beauteous landscape grew,
Opening like Canaan on rapt Israel's view.'

But even in those days of incandescent verse the judges found this a little too much, and Mr. Wentworth's epic ran not first, but second in the competition.

Now, in 1824, he was ready to go home. He knew exactly what he wanted—to become the most important man in the colony, and he thought he had the mental and physical equipment to become just that. But no longer would he lead as a member of the exclusive set. For some time past, both in his writing and in the vituperative and biting language that marked his public and private utterances, William Charles Wentworth had come right out on the side of the underdog.

It was impossible to separate his personal aspirations from his ambition to serve his native land—they were knit so closely that each complemented the other. For Wentworth, the only hope for Australia lay in obtaining constitutional freedom through an elected Parliament. He was intoxicated with the idea of Parliament. The House of Commons, in the long period of struggle leading up to the passing of the Reform Act, had witnessed some of the greatest debaters of all time, and Wentworth had listened entranced while such men as Canning, Huskisson and Peel led the battle against the diehards headed by Castlereagh.

But such eloquence could only reach the ears of the few admitted to the Chamber. He was going home to launch a public campaign, and suddenly the manner in which it could be started became clear in his mind. His friend Robert Wardell, though four years his junior, had already been proprietor and editor of a weekly paper, *The Statesman*; although he had been called to the Bar, like most ex-newspapermen he still sometimes had a yearning for the editorial chair. The stir caused by the successive editions of his book had impressed Wentworth with the power of the printed word. More than once he had asked Wardell, 'Why not come back with me?' And when he added, 'We might start a newspaper', the words made his friend sit up.

'Do you mean that seriously?'

Whether or not he had spoken with intent, Wentworth was certain in that moment that it was a magnificent idea. In a few hours *The Australian* was conceived by the union of two fertile minds, and the period known as 'the newspaper war' moved nearer.

The *Sydney Gazette* had been started by Governor King when, in 1803, he gave leave to an ingenious convict named George Howe, who managed the Government printing press, to collect material which, after being duly submitted for censorship, was published as a weekly newspaper. The *Gazette*, for which Howe was not only reporter and editor, but also typesetter, circulation manager, and delivery-man, was much in demand; as well as carrying official notices and advertisements, it chronicled the news of Sydney's budding social world. George Howe continued to run the paper under the successive naval Governors till Macquarie's arrival flooded the office with the new orders and proclamations from the Viceregal pen. By that time, Howe had the assistance of his son Robert, who took over from him in 1821. With the era of autocratic rule ending, that of the Freedom of the Press was due to begin.

Macquarie's successor, Sir Thomas Brisbane, certainly had no leanings towards despotism. It might have been better if he had, for he tended to leave everything to Major Frederick Goulburn, whom he had brought with him in the new post of Colonial Secretary, and the Major was given to altering his chief's orders and substituting his own. Sir Thomas was, above all, a man of peace. He was interested in science and astronomy and did not want to be embroiled in any kind of trouble. So when Wentworth and Wardell set up the printing press they had brought out from England in October, 1824, and three months later published the first issue of *The Australian*, he pronounced in favour of the new journal. Pushed by Major Goulburn, he did take legal advice, but it seemed that to interfere with the fire-eating young editors might land him in all sorts of difficulties. His own feeling was that the freedom of the press ought to be given a trial, and as far as he was concerned, the experiment was a success.

Governor Brisbane brought with him instructions to

push on with the exploration of the continent. Wentworth's book had already aroused great interest in Australia as a land of boundless opportunity for men working their own grants of land. The Bigge Report also encouraged the poor to take ship, though under rather different conditions, for a large section was devoted to a scheme for turning the whole of Australia into a country for the highly profitable export of fine wool. This was the plan to which John Macarthur had devoted the energies of a lifetime, and having 'nobbled' Mr. Bigge while the latter was collecting material for his Report, he had an unrivalled opportunity of putting forward his ideas in the fullest detail.

Macarthur considered that the colony should continue as a 'receptacle for convicts' suffering punishment appropriate to their crimes. Their rôle in life would be to serve as servants and shepherds for the *élite* ruling class, the owners of vast pasture lands grazing thousands of sheep. On these estates the peasants and convicts would grow grain for their own food which, added to a continuous supply of mutton from the inferior carcases, would make their support free of charge to the Government. Each year there would be more sheep, producing more profits, and needing more shepherds and cheap labour. What was to happen to those convicts who had served their sentences and earned their freedom was a problem which neither Mr. Macarthur nor Mr. Bigge had troubled to solve.

CHAPTER XI

THE RIDDLE OF THE RIVERS

WHETHER the country was going to be run by pastoral autocrats or rascally democrats, first it was necessary to open it up by exploration. Perhaps it was while indulging in his hobby of astronomy by gazing at the Australian sky that Sir Thomas Brisbane dreamed up his wonderful idea. Why not land a party of convicts on the extreme south coast and offer a full pardon to any that could make their way across the country to Sydney?

Sir Thomas himself had never tried to advance through virgin bush. The energetic young Australian-born Hamilton Hume, to whom he offered the charge of such a party, had enough experience of it to refuse the suggestion as made. However, he did offer to try and lead a party from Sydney to the south coast with William Hovell, a free settler, and on October 11th, 1824, the party set out, carrying their provisions in two carts drawn by teams of oxen.

They travelled fairly easily over fertile land till they were brought up short by a broad river called by the natives the Murrumbidgee. Several streams had been forded, but this one flowed too swiftly to take the risk. It was a challenge that Hume met by having the men cover the carts with tarpaulin. Behold, then, two 'punts', which floated long enough to enable Hume himself to swim the turgid river, towing the 'amphibious craft' by a rope held between his teeth. Such was the stuff of the pioneers. Encouraged by their leader, the other men and the oxen also made the swim.

But now the country became so rugged that they had to load the gear on to ox-back, and leave the carts behind. On they toiled, up and down, pushing and hacking through the everlasting trees. Far to the left they were amazed to see great snow-topped peaks towering into the sky—the Australian Alps, as they called them. At last they reached the banks of a clear and rapid stream; the Hume they named it, but now it is known as the Murray. Here was a problem: the oxen could not swim if fully laden, and they had abandoned the carts, so could not do as before and use them as punts. Ingeniously as the natives themselves, they constructed canoes of wicker-work, covered with the old tarpaulins.

Now the slopes were less heavily timbered. Two more rivers were discovered, one a splendid stream which they called the Hovell, later to be renamed the Goulburn after a man who had done nothing whatever to earn such a reward. Every day the party expected to come within sight of the open sea: each morning it seemed certain to happen the same afternoon or evening. At last, seeing a high peak in the distance, the two leaders left the party and with immense labour climbed the mountain—from its summit the Bass Strait would most certainly be visible. But all they could see were the everlasting gums, ridge after ridge fading into blue haze to the south. This peak has not had its name changed: Mount Disappointment they called it, for its bitter mockery of their hopes.

Consulting together, they decided they must be on the wrong course. Hovell had made the calculation, and in fact he had fixed their terminal point a whole degree too far East. This error threw all their reckoning out, and when a few days later they were overjoyed to see a large expanse of water, it was neither, as Hovell imagined, Westernport, nor Hume's choice of Port Phillip, but a new bay which the natives called Geelong. The dispute led to a bitter quarrel, each man heaping abuse and sarcasm on the other, and for the rest of the journey the two were scarcely on speaking terms.

Hume got the party back to Sydney without much difficulty. Both leaders were rewarded with grants of land, and the convicts with tickets of leave. Hovell still maintained that the bay they had seen, surrounded with land so beautiful that it was like a well-kept park, was Westernport. He was so insistent that Governor Brisbane sent him to found a settlement there. On arriving at the real Westernport, he soon found he had been wrong all the time, for that region was so ill-suited to settlement that within a year the enterprise was abandoned. 'More barren land,' reported Governor Brisbane of the country which was to become the richest dairying land in Australia.

From the summit of the Blue Mountains Wentworth and his companions had looked down over the rich plains which were to be called after Lord Bathurst. The two rivers watering this land, named after Macquarie and his son Lachlan, ran westward—but whither? In 1817, Surveyor John Oxley had followed the Lachlan for hundreds of miles through what he described as 'barren and desolate country' till the river finally lost itself in a series of marshes and stagnant pools; on another expedition along the Macquarie, the broad and rapid stream suddenly vanished into the earth.

What became of these rivers? Their disappearance seemed to confirm the old belief in a great inland sea to which they made their way underground. It was all very provoking, and destroyed the hope of a chain of inland waterways fit for navigation.

The problem became urgent after a three-year drought from 1825 on, which had shrivelled up the country. Charles Sturt, an officer of the newly-arrived 39th Regiment, became fascinated by the problem of the vanishing rivers. He suggested an expedition, and the Governor was only too happy to equip one; on December 7th, 1828, Sturt set out, accompanied by Hamilton Hume and eight convicts.

Sturt was no seeker of fame and fortune; his only wish was to contribute to the public good. The party followed the Macquarie to the point where Oxley had lost it in the marshes—but the drought had turned the bog to hard clay. In the hot, dead air, the scene was one of utter, lonely wretchedness. On horseback they pushed westward for a month over the dreary monotony of flat plains where the sun beat them like a flail, till they reached a deep gully.

Along the bottom, forty feet down, flowed a stream. The water was brackish, but good enough to water the horses. It was certain that in time of flood those deep banks sometimes held a raging river, and a long one, for they followed it for more than sixty miles before making their way back to Sydney. The river, which they named the Darling, solved one problem, for in its course it could receive the waters of all those rivers which were said to empty themselves into that mysterious inland sea.

In 1828, Sturt tried again. This time, with a naturalist named Macleay and eight convicts, he carried portable boats to the Murrumbidgee, and set off downstream in fine style. Beyond the junction with the Lachlan River the stream became narrow, surging through overhanging trees that shut off the light, over jutting snags and whirling rapids, till the skiff struck a root, twirled round, overturned, and sank.

From the whaler the men jumped out to salvage the stores—two anxious days it took them to recover everything they had lost.

A week after the start of the water journey, the boat suddenly shot out into a broad and noble river, emerging with such force that it almost hit the opposite bank. That river, which he named the Murray, was the same as that already crossed further up by Hume and Hovell. The first journey down this mighty river was full of excitement. From sunrise to dark they rowed, encamping for the night. The natives, as aborigines everywhere, were numerous and inquisitive. Their first reaction to strangers was always friendly, only after ill-treatment and when robbed of their property did they learn to hate the invaders who had stolen their land. Sturt, greeting them as friends, never suffered; instead they had fun together, especially when Macleay treated the natives to comic songs, which were a huge success.

Another beautiful stream flowed into the Murray from the north—the Darling, which they had already discovered. On the current they were borne west, then south till the stream became deeper and wider, spreading out into a broad sheet of water which they named Lake Alexandrina. But here, a terrible disappointment blasted their hopes.

They had planned to row through to the sea at Gulf St. Vincent (on which Adelaide now stands). Here it should be possible to find a ship to take them home, but the way to the sea was barred by a great bank of sand. No efforts could get them past it. For several days they tried everything, but Sturt realised that only one way was possible: to row back a thousand miles against a current so powerful that if they stopped to rest for a second they would be swept back a hundred yards!

The return up the Murray is one of the most heroic episodes in Australian history. Already the men were weak from fatigue and a low diet, and Sturt calculated that the rations would only last out if they took no longer getting back than they had taken travelling downstream. All would be well if they reached the food depot that had been left at the junction with the Murrumbidgee.

They rowed from dawn to dusk with an hour's rest at noon. Twenty-six days the journey out had taken; against the current, the tired, hungry rowers limped back in three days less—to find the depot had been pillaged, and they had to go on without the food on which they had yearningly fixed their thoughts.

For seventeen days more the weak and starving men struggled on in the midsummer heat, eyes glassy, minds beginning to wander. One man went mad, others lay down declaring they would rather die than row. With tremendous spirit Sturt got them through. On arrival in Sydney he went blind from nervous exhaustion, remaining in that state for several months. He had explored Australia's greatest river, and led the most important expedition yet into the interior. Sturt ranks with Flinders on the roll of Australian discoverers.

A full and Horrifying Account of a most dreadful

SHIPWRECK

Of the Neva, Convict Ship, Which sailed from Cork, for New South Wales, in May last, containing 241 Souls on Board, consisting of 150 female Convicts, 9 free Women, and 55 Children, all of whom perished except 6; and 9 of the Crew; with an Account of the dreadful Sufferings of those who were saved, while staying on a desert Island, being altogether one of the most heart-rending Accounts of Human Suffering which has occurred for a very long Period.

Title page of a broadsheet published in Cornwall in 1835

CHAPTER XII

THE NEWSPAPER WAR

THE first task of Colonel Ralph Darling, successor to Brisbane as Governor of New South Wales, was carried out before he had been officially inaugurated as Viceroy, for he was instructed to break his voyage at Hobart and there proclaim Van Diemen's Land a separate colony.

Sailing up the beautiful Derwent River on a December morning in 1825, Colonel Darling, as he contemplated the little town nestling at the foot of a great mountain, perhaps did not realise that it had been so placed to avoid surprise and massacre by bandits both black and white. The first convicts sent to Van Diemen's Land were the most ferocious of all the felons; escaping, they corrupted the aborigines, who soon became filled with intense hatred of all the invaders of their land, whether convicts or free men.

To dump large numbers of the world's most vicious characters on a barren shore, without sufficient guards to control them, was asking for trouble. They had to be free enough to work, and a determined man can release himself from almost any chains. Fleeing to the mountains, they joined the already hostile natives, who were much more warlike than the Australians; they taught them all the wickedness known to man, treating them like beasts or murdering them to suit their purpose. The ultimate horror was 'Hell's Gate'—Macquarie Harbour, where the worst of the worst were sent. On the stark west coast, lashed by Antarctic gales, where slopes clad in impenetrable bush ran straight down into the icy water, chain gangs toiled from dawn to dark. For punishment they were marooned for days on the rocks off-shore; many threw themselves into the sea as a release from their torment. Hell's Gate was the scene of callous brutality scarcely ever equalled in civilised times, surpassing anything in New South Wales. The few desperate men who managed to break away escaped into conditions of such utter bleakness that cases of cannibalism were not unknown.

For years the 'black war' went on against the aborigines and the bushrangers. The first Governor of the island who had any success in suppressing the marauders was Colonel Sorrell. A two-year gap between his rule and that of his successor allowed the bandits to regain their supremacy; under their leaders Crawford and Brady they kept the whole colony in a state of abject terror. Deep in the woods they lived secure; when soldiers blundered up the mountain tracks, they withdrew to refuges where no heavy boots could follow. In the end, Brady was captured by a young Australian-born bushman named John Batman, who lives in history for another reason which we shall see later.

By the time of Colonel Darling's visit, Governor Arthur had begun his twelve years of iron rule. For the first time, a prison had been built to confine the convicts—a grim fortress on the Tasman Peninsula the ruins of which are today a popular tourist attraction. Ancient horrors are exhibited by guides who describe with gusto how starving dogs were chained every few yards across the narrow isthmus which forms the sole land access to Port Arthur—the only alternative escape route to a plunge from the rocks into the raging sea.

Meanwhile, the island was attracting large numbers of settlers. Its temperate climate, unaffected by the droughts of the mainland, was ideal for sheep. Many men who arrived from England were ex-naval and military officers retired after the Napoleonic wars who, as reward for their services, had been given grants of land. In the mansions they built on their fertile acres, with as many assigned servants as they cared to apply for, these gentlemen enjoyed the gracious life of wealthy English squires, hunting, shooting, and fishing the magnificent rivers; for relaxation they and their ladies could ride or drive to the comfortable, well-planned towns of Hobart and Launceston. In the time of Governor Arthur, life in Van Dieman's Land could be pleasant indeed for a free man, and this term includes the many emancipated prisoners who were building up fortunes—among them a pint-sized spitfire known as John Pascoe Fawkner, licensee of the Cornwall Inn at Launceston, who was later to become co-founder with John Batman of the town of Melbourne.

The Governorship of Colonel Ralph Darling began quietly. The New South Wales convicts had become part of the local scene. Being the majority of the population, they filled every kind of post, for among their ranks were ex-officers, merchants, doctors, clerks, and lawyers (plenty of the latter), as well as skilled craftsmen and those assigned as servants to anyone who might need them. Now that the worst offenders had been banished to punishment centres, the floggings and hangings took place out of sight and earshot of Sydney society.

Macquarie had left a pleasant town with many graceful buildings as his memorial. A distinguished French officer visiting the town, which he had first seen sixteen years earlier, wrote: 'I had expected to see Sydney grown, but what was my astonishment to look upon the wonderful sight of an European city thriving in the bosom of a country all but wild.' On his voyage round the world, Sydney was the place that pleased the French officer most.

His new Excellency wrote to Lord Bathurst: 'So far I have never met with a more orderly and apparently better disposed set of people.' Little did he know his Sydneysiders!

The Governor had been warned in advance about John Macarthur. Though the Old Rebel was supposed to be in retirement, it was unthinkable that his fingers would not be in many pies, like the Bank he was founding that would be 'fit for gentlemen', in place of Macquarie's Bank of New South Wales. He was also promoting the Australian Agricultural Company, and talked of operating a newspaper, but this last idea never came to anything.

The trumpet-calls for democracy in Wentworth's *Australian* were even surpassed by the *Monitor*, property of firebrand Edward Smith Hall, who spent half his time in prison for seditious libel. But Wentworth's newspaper articles were only a part of his campaign for self-government. The first blow had been struck at a meeting to consider the farewell address to Sir Thomas Brisbane, when Wentworth had insisted on amendments demanding trial by jury as practised in Great Britain. There was no doubt that he regarded himself as future leader of the colony, and in the address of welcome to the new Governor he left that officer in no doubt either. 'Nothing will satisfy the colony,' Governor Darling was warned, 'but an effective Assembly, with taxation imposed only by elected members.'

His Excellency at first tried to conciliate Wentworth, inviting him to become a member of the new Legislative Council. But Wentworth rejected social status and respectability. He knew that the system of privilege could not last for ever, and he was obsessed with the desire to wreak vengeance on Macarthur and the Exclusives for the wound inflicted through his father on his own self-esteem. Words were his weapon, sarcastic and abusive, overwhelming his opponents with such floods of invective that few were willing to take him on in verbal combat. His demands were supported by facts and marshalled with all the skill of a brilliant lawyer. His personality towered above all others; ruthless and unscrupulous, he never wavered from his path to the goal of political freedom for his country.

Seeking a pretext to launch a campaign against established authority in the person of the Governor, Wentworth found one ready to hand.

For private soldiers of the regiments stationed in New South Wales, life was boring and pointless. There was no one with whom to fight a war that might bring glory and loot. Sydney provided no amusement beyond getting drunk, which often brought confinement or a flogging just as severe as that meted out to convicts. And just look how well a convict could do for himself after a few years, setting up in business or on a fine property, the soldiers told one another resentfully.

So one day towards the end of 1826, Joseph Sudds and Patrick Thompson, two disgruntled privates of the 57th Regiment, decided to promote themselves to the ranks of the convictry, reckoning that after a light sentence they too would become landowners and live in style. With this intention they walked into the nearest shop and, making sure they were noticed, stole a piece of calico. Grinning broadly, they were taken in charge and lodged in jail. In due course, they went before the magistrates, and the story of their intentions soon came out; rather unkindly, they thought, they were sentenced to seven years transportation, which meant an uncomfortable sojourn at Newcastle or Moreton Bay.

Governor Darling, however, decided to make an example of the two men. This had not been the first case of malingering to get out of the army, but he was determined that it should be the last. He caused a blacksmith to make two iron collars, each with two spikes projecting six inches or more, the whole weighing about fifteen pounds. Nothing like this had ever been seen in the colony before; the collars were, in fact, modelled on a barbarous punishment used for runaway slaves in the Indies. From the collars, heavy chains ran down to the wrists and ankles.

On November 26th, 1826, the entire regiment was drawn up on the barrack square. The two unfortunates were stripped of their uniforms, and clad in the yellow slops reserved for the lowest class of felons. The terrible iron collars were riveted round their necks and the chains fastened. Thus loaded, they were slowly paraded down the lines. Sudds, already sickly, had to be held up on each side as they were ceremonially drummed out of the regiment.

Governor Darling had altered the sentence from transportation to hard labour on the roads. Within a week Sudds was dead, and his companion was hastily released, as he was said to be losing his mind. The Governor realised that he had raised a hurricane.

"MURDERER!" was the epithet which the *Australian* hurled at the Governor. In the most violent language Wentworth and Wardell attacked him for interference and brutality. The *Gazette* sprang to his defence. Colonel Darling was ill-advised enough to enter personally into the vicious newspaper war which ensued, and soon the colony was divided into two factions, one extolling the Governor and the other denouncing him as the most brutal man on earth. Darling even resigned from the Turf Club, of which Wentworth was a member, letting it be known that every person in Government service would do well to do the same. He was an officious and self-opinionated man, but the days when a Governor could play the autocrat were past. Bluster did him no good: when it came to invective, Wentworth ranked high on the list of all-time champions, and in his newspaper and on public platforms he continued to inflame public opinion.

Now Darling moved to re-establish censorship. He had never approved of a free press, and so he tried to suppress the *Australian* by having a law passed by which newspapers could be published only under licence. But the Chief Justice refused to certify that such an act would not be 'repugnant to the laws of England'. However, the Judge could not block a measure which made a second conviction for publishing a libel 'tending to bring into contempt the Government of the colony' punishable by banishment for an unspecified period.

This threat caused Wentworth to relinquish his shares in the *Australian* to Wardell—banishment was something he could not risk. (Wardell passed them and his own on to the editor, who soon found himself in prison.) But the sympathies of Chief Justice Forbes were on Wentworth's side in his struggle for free institutions; for this was the basis of his whole campaign: that such freedom as Englishmen enjoyed by right in their own land should be made part of the constitution of Australia.

It was a slogan that might have caused wry amusement to some of those Englishmen at home, where the battle of the have-nots against the privileged few was at its height; where factory-owners threatened ruin if children were prevented from working sixteen hours a day, while women crawled in chains underground dragging hewn coal; whence in a few years the six Dorset labourers known as the Tolpuddle Martyrs would be transported to Van Diemens Land for daring to 'combine' with fellow workers in a Trade Union to demand a wage of 10s. a week.

The members of the Exclusive party were deeply alarmed at the headway being made by what seemed to them nothing but a gang of ex-convicts headed by a rabble-raiser. A memorandum was sent to Lord Bathurst attacking Wentworth by name, declaring that the agitation was being carried on by people without standing in the colony. Those who mattered had their own plans: John Macarthur's dream-scheme, which aimed at expansion in the form of vast properties owned by an *élite* and worked by convicts, was their favourite project.

Anniversary Day 1827 was the occasion of the largest meeting ever held in the colony. Parties rolled in from the limits of settlement in every sort of vehicle. Supported by Sir John Jamieson and other magnates who believed in self-government, Wentworth was as usual the leading spirit.

Working for Darling's impeachment as not being fit to govern, Wentworth seemed to be succeeding to Macarthur's mantle as a destroyer of Viceroys. It took him three years.

On the day when Colonel Darling finally sailed for England to answer a Parliamentary enquiry, Wentworth gave a great feast at his house in Vaucluse, overlooking Port Jackson. It was the apex of his career as a 'rabble leader'. Over four thousand people streamed along South Head to the place where sizzling bullocks and sheep hung in chains, roasting over great log fires. Thousands of loaves were ready, and drinks were on the house. All evening sports went on, bands played and Wentworth was carried around shoulder-high by his enthusiastic supporters.

As the ship bearing the recalled Governor sailed slowly down the harbour, his eyes rested on a blazing illumination:

"GOD SAVE THE KING AND DOWN WITH TYRANNY!"

For most of those who had celebrated that night, the news that Darling had not only been exonerated of all blame for his conduct in the colony, but had received the accolade of knighthood, was stale and devoid of interest by the time it trickled through to New South Wales. For now they had a new Governor who, for the first time, incredible as it may appear, was performing the miracle of pleasing almost everybody.

CHAPTER XIII

WEST- AND
SOUTHWARD-HO!

EVER since the crossing of the Blue Mountains, men had been pushing out from the coastal strip into new territory to the west, north, and south. We have already seen how, in 1824, Hume and Hovell crossed the Murrumbidgee and the Murray till from a peak they glimpsed the sea. Three years later, exploration began in earnest; though the developments in various parts of the continental coast extended over a number of years and overlapped one another in time.

There was, for instance, the story of the exploration of the Swan River as early as 1697 by a Dutch navigator, Vlamingh, who had penetrated some fifty miles up a large river on the western coast, to see hundreds of black swans sailing peacefully on its surface.

In 1826, a British naval officer named James Stirling was recalled from a long period of half-pay after the French Wars and sent to transfer some convicts from Melville Island in Australia's far north. Stirling had read of Vlamingh's voyage, and on reporting to Sydney he persuaded Governor Darling to send him to the west coast to try and locate the Dutchman's river. Like all explorers of the Australian unknown, Stirling had strange and excit-

Top: A drawing of Sydney Cove made by Captain John Hunter
seven months after Phillip's landing

Left: Commemoration stamp issued
in 1963. Wentworth is second from
the left

Bottom: Wentworth in early middle age.
From a contemporary portrait sketch

Top: Australia's wealth: Merinos on one of the large sheep farms in the southern table lands of New South Wales

Bottom: The Blue Mountains. A sheer 600-ft. drop at the 'Three Sisters', a rock formation at Echo Point

ing adventures in the search for his river. The black swans were still there; so were the stone-age aborigines. He returned to England so full of enthusiasm for the beauty and fertility of the country he had seen, that the Government sent out Captain Fremantle in H.M.S. *Challenger* to confirm British claims to the area south of the Swan River.

Governor Darling had for long been worrying about the unoccupied western coasts, so very vulnerable if the French or anyone else should take a fancy to them, and he had already sent Major Lockyer to occupy the point at the extreme south-west near where the town of Albany now stands. The then Prime Minister, Lord John Russell, when asked by a Frenchman how much of Australia British claimed, replied simply: 'The whole of it!' But at this time the British Government was having one of its economy fits and did not wish to embark on the foundation of another colony. The suggestion thrown out by Colonial Secretary Mr. Huskisson that the East India Company might care to finance the venture met with no response.

However, a group of Englishmen had been attracted by Stirling's glowing accounts of the Swan River, and Mr. Thomas Peel, a relative of the famous Sir Robert Peel, formed a syndicate to convey ten thousand emigrants to Western Australia at the cost of £30 a head. Thomas Peel and his partners were in it for the money, but he was also intrigued by the idea of making a great reputation as the founder of a new state.

Captain James Stirling was appointed Governor of this colony in cloud-cuckoo land. The whole venture was carried out in the vaguest possible way. On June 1st,

F

1829, the first fifty-five settlers were dumped on Garden Island, a sandy wilderness a few miles off the mouth of the Swan. With no conception of the utter desolation of the place, they had brought scarcely any of the necessary tools and provisions, so that they were more empty-handed than the stone-age men and with none of the skills the natives had evolved for themselves over the centuries.

Bitter winds blew in from the ocean as they crouched starving under brushwood shelters. Soon more ships carrying more hopeful immigrants arrived. Though some of these brought with them some seeds and tools, the experiment was a gigantic flop. The change from the English countryside was too unbelievably great. The settlers did not like Australia, and the Australians liked them still less; they attacked the intruders with spears, and were shot at with muskets in return. It was only through Stirling's energy and resourcefulness that Western Australia was not abandoned altogether, but he felt this was *his* colony and it was not going to die on his hands. He was thirty-eight, and he had brought out his twenty-two-year-old wife to be Governor's Lady; between them, with hard work, patience, and optimism, they kept the little settlement alive somehow.

Many of the settlers went home, back to England, where the experiment was described as 'the scarecrow of optimism'; some went off to try their luck elsewhere in Western Australia, but a few stuck it out. By 1850 the population of the settlement was only 5,886, and then an ironical solution of their problems was found . . . *convicts*!

It was ironical because everywhere else in Australia

transportation had, after an enormous struggle, been stopped. But labour was needed for roads and bridges and public works. Convicts and their guards would have to be fed, and this would provide a market for the produce of the settlers. The other states protested bitterly at this back-handed arrangement, but it achieved its purpose till 1868, when the scheme was abandoned. However, for many years far-away Western Australia was regarded as the Cinderella State.

Among the immigrants who had travelled eastward after their bad experience at Swan River had been the members of a family named Henty from Tarring in Sussex. Thomas Henty eventually settled in Tasmania; here he did well enough, but the stories his family heard from the whalers and seal traders of the rich country on the southern mainland tempted them to take ship and try their luck on a coast whereon till then no white man had set foot. In 1834, Edward, the sixth son, sailed over and established a farm successfully at a spot called Portland.

The Hentys were not the only settlers to be encouraged by the sealers' tales. One who was particularly attracted was John Batman, conqueror of the famous Brady Gang, of bandits, who had terrorised Van Diemen's Land. He had heard from his friend Hume something about the country on the other side of Bass Strait. Born a Sydney-sider, this gay and daring man had taken a farm in Tasmania, but saw little future in it. Everyone liked him, from the Governor down to the roughest bushman. With a group of friends he founded an association to investigate the Port Phillip district, and in May, 1835, with three servants and seven aborigines, he sailed north in his 15-ton schooner *Rebecca*. A fair-sized gale twice forced them back to port, but eventually, 'with Rebecca jumping like a kangaroo', they got across and through Port Phillip Rip, sailing up the great inland sea to Flinders's Indented Head. This, Batman felt certain, was the park-like country Hume had described to him, and the party lost no time in getting ashore.

Unlike the settlers from Britain, Australian-born white men did not think of the aborigines as savages. Growing up with dark people around them, often sharing their play with the carefree laughing children, they respected the aboriginal Australians and their tribal customs. The dark people might not have discovered the wheel, but they had evolved the boomerang, which would bring down a bird at three hundred feet or return to its owner's hand; they had no gunpowder, but the spear flung from a woomera could fly as straight and far as a musket ball. They could support themselves in country where a white man would soon die of hunger and thirst, and track a man or animal with a skill that was eerie.

John Batman had lived in the bush with aborigines, and few white men knew as much as he of their intricate customs. So when one day some members of the Dutigalla tribe approached him with menacing gestures, he felt sure that he could stop the threatened assault by producing the usual presents of looking-glasses and beads. But they did not seem pacified at all.

At this juncture extraordinary good luck for Batman arrived in the person of a very tall man, whose filthy skin was nevertheless lighter than that of his companions from the bush, and whose stumbling words were unmistakably English. 'Buckley's chance' was before them in the flesh—the convict William Buckley, who had escaped from Collins's party thirty-three years earlier to live with the natives! He turned out to be a very useful intermediary, and the result of the encounter was a quite extraordinary 'treaty'.

Batman had embarked on this journey with the draft of a document. Joseph Tice Gellibrand, the legal brain behind the Port Phillip Association, had drawn up a 'Deed of Conveyance' for the purchase of land, and on June 6th, 1835, a meeting was held between Batman and eight chiefs who between them were reputed to own the whole of the territory of that district, which they called Geelong.

Batman wrote in his Journal:

After some explanation by Buckley, I purchased two large tracts of land from them, about 600,000 acres, and delivered over to them blankets, knives, looking-glasses, tomahawks, beads, scissors, flour etc. as payment and agreed to give them a tribute or rent yearly for ever. The parchment the eight chiefs signed this afternoon... Just before leaving, the two principal chiefs came and brought their two cloaks or royal mantles and laid them at my feet. On my consenting to take them, they placed them round my neck and shoulders and seemed quite pleased to see me walking about with them on.

The actual 'treaty', which the aborigines Jagajaga, Cooloolock, Bungarie, Yanyan, Moowhip and Manmarmalar 'signed' in triplicate, was long and detailed, setting out the exact purchase price (e.g. twelve pairs of scissors, fifty handkerchiefs etc.) The idea of savages who had never before even seen writing agreeing that 'we, our heirs and successors give, grant, enfeoff and confirm unto the said John Batman' a vast tract of land, may seem absurd; but as far as the other settlements made by the British in Australia were concerned, the invaders did not pay the owners of the land the courtesy of asking their permission; they just moved in and took possession.

Next morning being Sunday, the new landowner explored a small part of his property, walking round what is now the suburb of North Melbourne. To reach this district he had gone up the Yarra River in his boat. The words he wrote in his journal that evening have become history; the last sentence is let into the pavement of the great city of Melbourne near the approximate place where it was written: 'About six miles up found the river all good water and very deep. This will be the place for a village.'

Batman's claim to be Melbourne's founder was hotly disputed by ugly little Johnny Pascoe Fawkner, licensee of the Cornwall Inn at Launceston. As the son of a convict father, Fawkner had, like Buckley, been in Collins's unsuccessful settling party at Port Phillip thirty-three years earlier, and had later himself served a prison sentence. He was a member of the Port Phillip Association formed to 'pirate' the forbidden land, and when Batman, weary but triumphant, strode into Fawkner's bar announcing, 'I am the greatest landowner on earth', Fawkner made plans to get across the Strait as soon as his debts would permit. (It is part of the fascinating nearness of Australian history that a man of 70 recently told how as a boy he heard this story from someone who, in his own boyhood, had been present at that scene).

Fawkner, with a large party, was soon landing on the shores of Port Phillip. A better businessman than Batman, quarrelsome and aggressive as a terrier, he was a true founder of Melbourne; in four years Batman was dead, and soon Fawkner was the leading citizen—innkeeper, newspaper proprietor, councillor, and member of the Legislative Assembly.

But when in 1835 his party arrived in the Yarra river, he was met by representatives left behind by Batman, and told: 'Trespassers will be prosecuted!' In fact, as soon as the news reached Sydney, Governor Bourke issued a proclamation forbidding anybody to 'invade the vacant Crown Land'. But even before this proclamation arrived, settlers had begun to establish themselves on large claims, and a new town was rising. Some, thinking of the treaty with the Chiefs, said it ought to be called 'Batmania'.

The whole process of colonising Australia had hitherto been haphazard in the extreme. The original convicts were dumped on a coast of which nothing was known at all. Sub-colonies had been scratched on Norfolk Island and in Van Diemen's Land. Collins's attempt at founding a settlement at Port Phillip, in waterless scrub country, had failed altogether. Swan River had indeed been organised in London, but on such false premises that the immigrants had suffered terrible privations.

By the time of the disappointments of Swan River, however, the feeling in England about colonisation had undergone a change. With the advance of the Industrial Revolution there were more people than jobs, and while this was fine for employers, the workers became more restive than ever under their miserable conditions. Emigration seemed a solution, and much interest was aroused

Female Emigration

TO

AUSTRALIA.

COMMITTEE:

EDWARD FORSTER, Esq. *Chairman.*
SAMUEL HOARE, Esq.
JOHN TAYLOR, Esq.
THOMAS LEWIN, Esq.
S. H. STERRY, Esq.

CHARLES HOLTE BRACEBRIDGE, Esq.
JOHN S. REYNOLDS, Esq.
JOHN PIRIE, Esq.
CAPEL CURE, Esq.
WILLIAM CRAWFORD, Esq.

CHARLES LUSHINGTON, Esq.
JOHN ABEL SMITH, Esq. M.P.
GEORGE LONG, Esq.
COLONEL PHIPPS,
NADIR BAXTER, Esq.
CAPTAIN DANIEL PRING, R.N

The Committee for promoting the Emigration

OF

Single Women

To AUSTRALIA, acting under the Sanction of His Majesty's Secretary of State for the Colonies, HEREBY GIVE NOTICE, That

THE SPLENDID TEAK-BUILT SHIP

"*David Scott,*" *of 773 Tons Register,*

Carrying an experienced Surgeon, and a respectable Person and his Wife as Superintendents to secure the Comfort and Protection of the Emigrants during the Voyage, will sail from

on Thursday 10th of July next,

(Beyond which day she will on no account be detained) direct for

SYDNEY.

Single Women and Widows of good Character, from 15 to 30 Years of Age, desirous of bettering their Condition by Emigrating to that healthy and highly prosperous Colony, where the number of Females compared with the entire Population is greatly deficient, and where consequently from the great demand for Servants, and other Female Employments, the Wages are comparatively high, may obtain a Passage

on payment of FIVE POUNDS only.

Those who are unable to raise even that Sum here, may, when approved by the Committee, go *without any Money Payment whatever*, as their Notes of Hand will be taken, payable in the Colony within a reasonable time after their arrival, when they have acquired the means to do so: in both cases the Parties will have the advantage of the **Government Grant** in aid of their Passage.

The Females who proceed by this Conveyance will be taken care of on their first Landing at Sydney. They will find there a List of the various Situations to be obtained, and of the Wages offered, and will be perfectly free to make their own Election; they will not be bound to any person, or subjected to any restraint, but will be, to all intents and purposes, perfectly free to act and decide for themselves.

Females in the Country who may desire to avail themselves of the important advantages thus offered them, should apply by Letter to "The Emigration Committee, London," under Cover addressed to "The UNDER SECRETARY OF STATE, COLONIAL DEPARTMENT, LONDON." It will be necessary that the Application be accompanied by a Certificate of Character from the Resident Minister of the Parish, or from some other respectable Persons to whom the Applicant may be known; but the Certificate of the Resident Minister is in all cases most desirable. Such Females as may find it expedient may, when approved by the Committee as fit persons to go by this Conveyance, be boarded temporarily in London, prior to Embarkation, on Payment of 7s. per Week.

☞ All Applications made under cover in the foregoing manner, or personally, will receive early Answers, and all necessary Information, by applying to

JOHN MARSHALL, Agent to the Committee, 26, Birchin Lane, Cornhill, London.

EDWARD FORSTER, *Chairman.*

NOTE.—The Committee have the satisfaction to state that of 217 Females who went out by the "Bussorah Merchant," 180 obtained good Situations within three Days of their Landing, and the remainder were all well placed within a few Days, under the advice of a Ladies' Committee, formed in the Colony expressly to aid the Females on their arrival.

LONDON; 1st May, 1834.

By Authority:

PRINTED BY JOSEPH HARTNELL, FLEET STREET, FOR HIS MAJESTY'S STATIONERY OFFICE.

Handbill published by H.M. Stationery Office, 1834

when in 1829 a little book was published under the title, *A Letter from Sydney*.

This was written in such lively style that everyone imagined the author, Edward Gibbon Wakefield, had written it from personal experience on the spot, but actually he had never been out of England. The letter was not only lively, it seemed to make sense as well. Soon he had quite a following of people who believed he had worked out a way of founding and developing a colony on fool-proof lines.

Wakefield argued that land should not be given away, but sold 'always at a sufficient price'. If, he said, land is too cheap, men will not go on working for settlers, for they will soon save enough to buy land of their own; so there will be no reliable supply of labourers. Settlers with capital will not come out unless there is labour to work their properties.

Therefore, a new colony must have two things: first a fund with which labour can be brought out from the home country where there is too much of it; secondly, a means of keeping such people in the position of labourers once they arrive in the colony.

So, the *Letter* went on, if you sell colonial land not cheaply, as was done at Swan River, but 'at a sufficient price' to enable you to bring out with the proceeds of the sales all the labour the colonists require, you will maintain an exact balance between the land you wish to have occupied, the capital necessary to develop it, and the labour required to work it. Labourers will have to remain labourers for two or three years before they can save up enough to buy land; and the price they will have to pay will enable you to obtain a constant flow of fresh labour from the abundant supply in England—provided that the proceeds of land sales are used for no other purpose than paying for emigration.

By following up his book with numerous newspaper articles, Wakefield aroused so much interest that a Colonisation Society was formed; and in that very year, the news arrived of Charles Sturt's great discoveries of good land round the Murray. An experiment was made —and the result was the State of South Australia.

But it had been private employers who were so interested, not the Government, which was still opposed to expansion in Australia. A chief official wrote that the Secretary of State 'does not feel at liberty to hold out any encouragement to schemes which have for their object the extension of the number of His Majesty's settlements abroad which . . . are always liable to end in becoming a source of expense to the revenue of this country'. However, the Government eventually agreed that under a Governor appointed by the Crown a new colony should be founded, to which the transportation of convicts should be barred altogether. According to the usual custom, it appointed an honest old naval officer, Captain Hindmarsh, to the post of Governor, which was to need an administrator of genius.

Despite so much argument and theoretical preparation, no one had troubled to find out the best site for the first settlement. It was the Swan River muddle all over again. In July, 1836, at the beginning of the southern winter, two shiploads of immigrants were landed on Kangaroo Island, which Flinders had so touchingly described as the dying ground for pelicans. They even got there before the surveying party led by Colonel Light who, on arrival, immediately decided that a pelicans' cemetery was no place for an infant colony, and went off to search for something better.

Today a park above the beautiful city of Adelaide is called 'Light's vision'. From a pedestal a bronze figure looks out over the city which the Colonel planned against enormous opposition; for Governor Hindmarsh, when he arrived four months later, was highly displeased with Light's choice of a site seven miles from the sea. In fact, following the usual pattern, the Governor and the Commissioners of the South Australia Company disagreed about everything, and within eighteen months he was on his way home, to be succeeded by Colonel George Gawler, another gallant officer who was no master mind.

Poor Gawler arrived to find no money in the safe, salaries unpaid, and debts falling due—an unpleasant welcome for a new Governor. He was distracted. All around him were creditors clamouring for their money. In all the beautifully worked out Wakefield Plan, no one had taken into account the eternal human desire to get rich quick without working for it. Instead of cultivating the land, buyers had gambled in real estate; a land boom set in while the imported labourers were standing about with no work and no wages.

What was the poor Governor to do? What he did was to issue Government Bills, which people believed to be as good as cash. The Commissioners kept sending out more immigrants. By 1841, 299,000 acres had been sold, but only 2,500 acres were under cultivation.

Came the inevitable crash. To enable the unemployed labourers to eat, Gawler had undertaken extensive public works. Bridges, buildings, and harbour works were going up in the settlement that had started from scratch, all paid for with Government Bills. When the reckoning came, the Governor had overspent his revenue to the tune of £291,000. The Government refused to pay, and the bubble burst.

So Colonel Gawler joined the growing band of Governors broken by Australia, though a Committee of the House of Commons later admitted that they did not see how else he could have acted, and at the time of his departure no one could suggest what to do next. But the dire need brought forth the right man, in the surprising person of a handsome statesman aged just twenty-eight, Captain George Grey.

Captain Grey arrived in May, 1841, stepping off the ship with a despatch informing Colonel Gawler that he was dismissed and that he was to succeed him. Grey was an astonishing young man. His remarkable explorations in South Australia, entailing great privations, had caused Lord John Russell to appoint him Governor. He cleaned up the colony's murky finances in just under five years.

It was a thankless task. He had to rescue the floundering, bankrupt settlement and place it on a sound footing. He did it by insisting that Parliament should wipe out the obligations incurred by Gawler's Bills—altogether £405,000. Reluctantly, the Government took its medicine. By practising the most rigid economy, Grey averted ruin, and by the beginning of 1843, South Australia had staggered to its feet and was ready for a new start.

A period of austerity is never much appreciated. Grey was unpopular with his tight-fisted subjects, but he took absolutely no notice of their moans. At the end of his term, the Prime Minister told the House of Commons that 'in the years of his administration he had solved the problem with a degree of energy and success which could scarcely be expected of anyone. He has extricated the colony, and gained the goodwill of both settlers and aboriginals'.

George Grey was rewarded by being appointed Governor of New Zealand—itself no easy task at that time.

The appointment in 1828 of Major Livingstone Mitchell, Peninsular War veteran, as Surveyor-General of New South Wales was well overdue, for the land position in the colony was in utter confusion. Ever since Governor Phillip had granted one acre to Australia's first farmer, James Ruse, tracts of land had been handed out to individuals, from 30-acre plots to ex-convicts up to the thousands of acres owned by shepherd kings like Macarthur and Samuel Marsden. Rich settlers used to arrive from England with 'grants' from their patrons which, when confirmed by a harrassed Governor, were often not cultivated but sold and re-sold for profit. The first so-called Surveyor-General, John Oxley, was an ex-naval officer who had neither training for his post nor interest in it.

Once the country beyond the Blue Mountains was open, it seemed that there was so much land that it was scarcely necessary to worry about boundaries. When the Australian Agricultural Company, a brain child of John Macarthur, was founded by Act of Parliament in 1824, it obtained 500,000 acres free of charge, and the era of the 'squatters' began.

In America, a squatter was a person who entered land

for which he had no title. The Australian term was first applied to 'someone who went out into unoccupied land and without official sanction built a hut or pastured his sheep or cattle'. Around 1815, the word commonly denoted runaway convicts or ticket-of-leave men who had as like as not stolen their livestock. But gradually squatting became respectable, till the 'squattocracy' began to be looked upon as the highest class. Owners of great flocks had to have pastures. The London Government had no settled policy; in little England nobody could imagine half a million square miles of fertile land ready for the taking. As Governor Gipps wrote later: 'As well try to confine the Arabs within a circle traced on the sand as to confine the graziers and wool growers of New South Wales within bounds that can possibly be assigned to them.'

Something had to be done, and in 1836 Governor Bourke devised a plan of dividing the land occupied by squatters into pastoral districts, granting licences to the occupants of 'runs', for which they were charged according to how many sheep a run would graze. This suited the squatters and gave them, for the time being, a sense of security.

Major Mitchell on his arrival had found a country where the spirit of self-reliant Australianism was slowly asserting itself against a background of privilege and intrigue. The land situation was calling urgently for an orderly survey. However, Thomas Livingstone Mitchell, 'the Major' as he was commonly called, had more taste for exploration than for an office desk. He was a difficult man, quarrelsome and quick to take offence. Of Charles Sturt he was extremely jealous, and could scarcely contain his annoyance when that officer, junior to himself, had been selected to solve the problem of the rivers. But there was still plenty of country waiting to be explored in 1831, and with a party of fifteen convicts he set out for the north-west, where he reached Sturt's upper Darling and linked up two previously half-traced rivers. Neither did a second expedition accomplish much —two of his men were speared by natives, the stores plundered, and the Major returned to Sydney in a very disgrunted frame of mind. For a time he settled down to his neglected desk work.

The eccentric Surveyor-General seemed to get in everyone's hair, and there was general satisfaction when, in 1836, he was sent by the Governor to find out whether the Darling was really the river which Sturt had found flowing into the Murray. After confirming that this was indeed so, Mitchell, desperate to explore some place where another man had not already preceded him, took his party (twenty-five convicts this time) across the mighty Murray and climbed a mountain to view the country ahead.

What he saw was a revelation, as dazzling as the view from the Blue Mountains over which Wentworth had gone into such ecstacies. Mitchell was almost as lyrical in his description:

As I stood, the first intruder on the sublime solitude of those verdant plains as yet untouched by flocks or herds, I felt conscious of being the harbinger of mighty changes there; for our steps would soon be followed by the men and animals for whom it seemed to have been prepared.

Alas, Thomas Livingstone Mitchell had once again come

second. After passing the slopes of the Grampians and following the River Glenelg, where lush creepers swept into the eddying current, the Major began his homeward route. Gazing towards the coast, he saw a schooner lying anchored in the bay. On the shore nestled a neat homestead, surrounded by cocks and hens, sheep, goats, and cows. The garden bloomed with fruit and vegetables. Except for the vine, nothing could have been more like England transported to this uninhabited Eden.

Mitchell had, of course, come upon the settlement established by the Hentys nearly two years earlier. These pioneers were surprised and delighted to see him, and did everything in their power to entertain him—even a whale-hunt was laid on, for while he was enjoying their hospitality a hump-backed whale entered the bay. It is amusing to think of the intrepid explorer who had imagined himself the discoverer of virgin country 'witnessing from a verandah on a beautiful afternoon at Portland Bay all the wondrous perils of harpooners and whaleboats of which I had delighted to read in scenes of the stormy north'.

So now the secret was out of what was happening in the fertile country soon to become the State of Victoria, for the Major also took back tidings of Batman's infant 'village' 230 miles along the coast at Port Phillip which, unknown and unauthorised, was more than a year old. In Sydney the news caused wild excitement, and the rich grazing plains had not long to wait before the flock-masters were on the way.

There were three main currents of men and stock, their speed cut to the walking pace of cows and sheep: one stream went north to the Liverpool Plains and Darling

PUBLIC
DINNER
TO
Mʀ HAWDON

A number of persons having expressed a desire to testify their sense of the spirited and enterprizing conduct of **Mr. HAWDON** in bringing **CATTLE** overland from *New South Wales* to *Adelaide*, it is proposed

THAT A
PUBLIC DINNER

Shall be given to that gentleman, and that a
PIECE OF PLATE

Shall be presented to him in commemoration of the event, and as a Testimony of the feeling of the Colonists.

Persons desirous of evincing their sentiments are invited to record their Names in a paper left for this purpose at the POST OFFICE.

N. B. An early day will be fixed for the **DINNER**, of which due notice will be given.

Adelaide, 4th May, 1838.

Printed at the office of the *Southern Australian*.

Joseph Hawdon was the first 'overlander' to bring cattle from New South Wales to Adelaide in April, 1838

Downs in what was to become Queensland, explored by Alan Cunningham in 1827; others struck south across the Murray to Port Phillip and Mitchell's 'Australia Felix'; and the third stream went south-east to the dairying country which, in honour of a later Governor, would become known as Gippsland.

Dirty and rough they often were, riding on to find the best country, always afraid they would miss something better further on with more water and sweeter grass. Some went alone, prospecting ahead on horseback to stake a claim, returning to fetch their stock; but that was a gamble, for who would respect that blaze on the trees, the anti-trespassers notice that said in effect 'This land is mine. KEEP OUT!'

CHAPTER XIV

'UNLOCK THE LAND!'

THE successor to Governor Darling added the talent and energy of Macquarie to a frank and cordial manner—a combination which won the colonists' hearts so that long after his term had ended he was spoken of as 'Good old Governor Bourke'.

Taking over as Viceroy in 1831, Lieutenant-General Sir Richard Bourke was faced with the chaos of land grants. The ingenuity and tact with which he devised what was called 'a very fair arrangement' set the pattern of the popular Governorship which was to prevail for the next few years.

This honeymoon period coincided with a change in the personality of William Wentworth. He was now a very rich man. In addition to his own property and earnings at the Bar, the death of his father had made him a great landowner. The fury that had bedevilled him ever since the discovery of his parent's early lapse from grace had diminished now that by his own efforts he had become the most influential man in the colony. Democratic fevers of youth gave way to the outlook of the rich pastoral employer wishing to get cheap labour.

The new Governor, of course, knew all about the part Wentworth had played in the displacement of Sir Ralph Darling, and must have looked forward with mixed feelings to his first encounter with the redoubtable leader whom he invited to Government House. However, the two men got on well together. Bourke, though the King's representative, could fully sympathise with Wentworth's ambitions for his country. Wentworth's own feelings were shown when he accepted Sir Richard's invitation to become a magistrate. Hitherto he had refused to sit on the Bench for fear of losing his independence; but the acceptance of this sign of conventional respectability did not stop his work to bring responsible government nearer.

The British Government had rejected the Petition presented after the great meeting of Anniversary Day, 1827, though giving in to the extent of enlarging the Legislative Council (first set up in 1823, with 'not more than 7 nor fewer than 5 members appointed by the Crown'); creating an Executive Council; and granting emancipists as well as others the right of serving on juries.

At the Anniversary Day meeting of 1833, Wentworth went even further. By an attack on the Sheriff, he virtually destroyed the power of the Government to control the conduct of public assemblies and to censor their proceedings. Despite the opposition of the Macarthur faction, he secured the adoption of a reinforced version of the rejected Petition of 1827, which was in due course presented to the House of Commons. Backing that presentation was the news of the formation of the 'Australian Patriotic Association', pledged to fight to the death for responsible government. To Members of Parliament, still reeling from the struggles of the Reform Act, the ghosts of the Boston Tea Party and the American War of Independence must have walked again.

But though still the leader of the radical party, Wentworth's own views were changing, largely through the events taking place in Australia itself. He was coming to believe that persons were not entitled to political power merely because they were determined to throw off oppression. Many such people, he argued now, were simply not capable of forming intelligent opinions; in fact, the under-privileged were so by their own fault; therefore, those who had done well for themselves, to wit the squatters and pastoralists, were the people best qualified to possess power. He had been driven into democracy by sour grapes—he was at heart a Whig, never a Republican. So, for the second time in his life, Wentworth's thinking was completely reversing itself in so far as it concerned the best means to reach his goal of responsible self-government. But for that he still had a long way to go.

To Wentworth it was a personal sorrow when Sir Richard's term as Governor ended. In his speech of farewell, he worked up the feelings of the crowd to such a pitch that £700 was subscribed on the spot towards the erection of a statue to remember him by. The statue which today stands in front of the Public Library of New South Wales has a long inscription on the plinth, doubtless drafted by one who was as extravagant in praise as in blame. Besides expressing the colonists' affection, it gives a good idea of the conditions in Australia during that period, in which Australia's population had risen from 48,000 to 87,000:

This statue of Lieutenant General Sir Richard Bourke, K.C.B. is erected by the people of New South Wales to record his able, honest and benevolent administration from 1831 to 1837. Selected for the Government at a period of singular difficulty, his judgment, urbanity and firmness justified the choice. Comprehending at once the vast resources peculiar to this colony, he applied them for the first time systematically to its benefit. He voluntarily divested himself of the prodigious influence arising from the assignment of penal labour and enacted just and salutary laws for the administration of penal discipline. He was the first Governor who published satisfactory accounts of public receipts and expenditure. Without oppression or detriment to any interest he raised the revenue to a vast amount and from its surplus realised extensive plans of immigration. He established religious equality on a just and firm basis and sought to provide for all without distinction of sect a sound and adequate system of national education. He constructed various public works of permanent utility. He founded the flourishing settlement of Port Phillip and threw open the unlimited wilds of Australia to pastoral enterprise. He established Savings banks and was the patron of the first Mechanics' Institute. He created an equitable tribunal for determining upon claims to grants of land. He was the warm friend of the liberty of the press. He extended trial by jury after its almost total suspension for many years. By these and numerous other measures for the moral, religious and general improvement of all classes he raised the colony to unexampled prosperity, and retired amid the reverent and affectionate regret of the people, having won their confidence by his integrity, their gratitude by his services, their admiration by his public talents and their esteem by his public works.

To follow a Governor who had gained such affection was the misfortune of Sir George Gipps who, though a conscientious and able man, had no pretensions to the Bourke charm. The fact that he was as unpopular as his predecessor had been loved, was largely due to the fact that he had to uphold the authority of the British Colonial Office against the increasingly powerful Legislative Assembly led by Wentworth, who did not cease to use every weapon in his armoury against the Governor.

Though Wentworth and Sir George were men who had little in common, Gipps recommended his appointment to the Legislature in 1839, describing him as 'a man of vast influence as well as vast possessions'. However, the Governor withdrew his support after the extraordinary episode when Wentworth tried to buy New Zealand!

Early in 1840, seven Maori chiefs arrived in Sydney, creating much interest with their tattooed faces and outlandish dress. The Governor invited them to acknowledge Queen Victoria as their sovereign ruler. With a gift of ten sovereigns each, they went off, promising to come back and sign a declaration.

When they did not return, Gipps discovered that Wentworth and some of his associates had 'purchased' 200,000 acres of North Island and part of South Island, totalling 20,000,000 acres 'for £200 in ready money with a promise of like sum per annum as long as they shall live'. Such a transaction made Batman's 'treaty' of Port Phillip look like a deal in peanuts.

Furious, Gipps refused to sanction the purchase. 'Talk of jobbery!' he cried angrily. 'If all the corruption that has defiled England since the time of the Stuarts were to be herded into one heap it would not make such a sum as this! Mr. Wentworth asks me to lend a hand in perpetrating a sale that grants him twenty millions of acres at the rate of one hundred acres for one farthing.' He pointed out that although the Red Indians sold Connecticut for some old coats, the N.S.W. Government had no reason to acknowledge similar purchases in New Zealand.

Wentworth never forgave Gipps for thwarting one of the most audacious land-grabbing attempts in history. He resigned his commission as magistrate and separated himself from any official connection with the Government. However, the time was coming when no personal quarrels could prevent him from taking his part in making his country's laws, for the arrival of representative government was close at hand.

From the beginning, everything had gone against Gipps. There was a six-year drought, when emaciated sheep were sold for 6d apiece or boiled down for tallow; a financial crisis from over-speculation in land ruined thousands more; and worst of all, the transportation of convicts was discontinued.

In 1837, a Committee of the House of Commons had examined the whole question of transportation and came up with a report that scandalised the nation—a thousand pages telling of horror and cruelty, of dreariness and misery. Transportation had cost Britain up to £500,000 a year for half a century. As a result of the report, an Order in Council was passed to the effect that no more convicts should be sent to the Australian mainland, though they could still be sent to Norfolk Island and Van Dieman's Land.

This course was to have two disturbing effects. With no improved prison system at home, it meant that for several years almost the whole criminal population of Great Britain was poured into Van Diemen's Land, where the situation became disastrous indeed.

With about four thousand felons a year flooding into the little island, people who had built up farms and industries were ruined. The criminals were cocks of the walk, with their own newspaper which even suggested that it would be a good thing to 'kick the free settlers out of the colony altogether!' The unhappy Governor to be landed with this avalanche of jailbirds was Sir John Franklin, the great and gallant Arctic explorer who had sailed as a midshipman in Flinders's *Investigator*. His struggle to make ferocity and humanity run in double harness ended inevitably in failure, but a failure which finally led to the abandoning of the system altogether. In 1853, the island was given self-government, and three years later the hated name of Van Diemen's Land, with all the horrors it stood for, was abandoned. Under the name of Tasmania the little colony embarked on a new life.

The effect on the Australian mainland of the ending of transportation was to deprive the pastoralists of their cheap and plentiful labour, and this was the issue which brough the two faction leaders James Macarthur and Wentworth on to the same platform. One might have thought that such a decision would have warmed the heart of one who had fought so hard for the rights of ex-convicts, but a scheme to deprive the country of cheap labour was not one to appeal to a landowner and large employer. Wentworth was now a family man, having married a young woman named Sarah Cox, a blacksmith's daughter who had helped him in his rabble-raising days and was now presenting him with sons and daughters to found the dynasty he had dreamed of.

Many emancipists who had made their pile were now themselves in favour of transportation, and opposed the humane efforts being made by the United Kingdom. Howls of rage were going up from the outraged squattocracy. Agitation meetings were held, where one rich wool-grower voiced the sentiments of all with the words: 'I do not care to be ruined for virtue's sake!' But the less wealthy, the poor free settlers who wished to sell their labour, were delighted with the altered situation.

The whole character of the population was changing. The struggle was no longer a social one of exclusives versus emancipists, but of rich against poor. The new free immigrants disapproved of the great estates and cared nothing for the old disputes. To them there was no choice between Wentworth and Macarthur as grinders of the faces of the poor. Many were chartists, who had come from England to a country where they had expected to find plenty of room. The cry was going up, 'Unlock the land!', and their emerging leader was young Henry Parkes.

This son of a poor English farmer had arrived in Sydney in 1839. After doing various menial jobs he set himself up as an ivory turner, making billiard balls and chessmen, and was soon a fiery figure in local politics. As the career of William Wentworth approached its zenith and subsequent decline, that of the future Prime Minister Sir Henry Parkes, architect of Australia's Federation, was just beginning.

With his new ally James Macarthur, Wentworth fought the British Government's scheme to end transportation; or, if there were to be no more convicts, he expressed himself ready to accept the importation of coolies from Asia to work the land. Now it was time for howls from the labouring classes against one who, as his own brain-child, *The Australian*, wrote, 'first taught this colony what liberty could be, but has since betrayed them'.

Meanwhile he had drafted two Bills for consideration at Westminster. The first was rejected, but the second, seeking a single House of 50 members, one-fifth nominated and the rest elected on a property franchise, was accepted in modified form in an Act of 1842. This provided for a Legislative Council of 36 members, of whom 6 officials and 6 civilians were to be appointed by the Crown, and 24 elected on a property qualification. However, the legislative and executive functions were still restricted through the vesting in the Governor of the permanent revenue of the colony, and in the Secretary of the Colonies of the authority to fix the salaries of certain officials.

Wentworth had refused the urging of three Governors to be nominated to the old Council. Now, as one of the richest men in the country, he was freely elected on a property franchise—though he did not achieve his ambition to head the House as Speaker. After 25 years of agitation, he was now fifty-two. In the following year he began the last phase of the struggle.

Any new experiment in legislature launched during a 6-year drought could expect trouble. Most of the work with which he strengthened his position was in the interest of saving the squatting and pastoral interests from bankruptcy. With the masses, however, his popularity plummetted down.

In England itself great difficulties were being experienced, as there was no way of lodging the volume of human frailty that had formerly been shipped abroad. So a new formula was thought up: prisoners should serve a short sentence at Pentonville or Millbank and then, as presumably reformed characters, be landed in Australia, free to roam about at will, provided they did not return to England. A scream of rage went up all over the colony at a prospect which would give such delinquents even more liberty than a ticket-of-leave man compelled to report at regular intervals.

The settlers at Port Phillip had always protested vigorously against the landing of convicts in their district. After several shiploads of 'reformed characters' had been dumped there, local feeling became so explosive that when the *Randolph* anchored off Melbourne, the captain was compelled by threats of armed resistance to take her up to Sydney. But when later the *Hashemy* arrived in Port Jackson, the Sydneysiders too were determined not to admit the loathed cargo. At a great public meeting in pouring rain, Henry Parkes, in his apron and workman's cap, inflamed the crowd with his eloquence. Shops were closed, and the angry mob converged on Government House.

Through the efforts of Parkes, the convicts were prevented from landing, and the *Hashemy* took her wretched cargo on to Brisbane. The incident led to the formation of the anti-Transportation League, and Wentworth's popularity sank to a new low. Even by his long-devoted followers he was now branded 'turncoat', ally of the rich

LIST OF THE

Traitors,—Trimmers,—Rose-water Liberals,—and Political Tidewaiters, who voted for **MR. WENTWORTH'S ARTFUL DODGE**, the adjournment of the Question of **NO TRANSPORTATION!!!** in the Legislative Council of New South Wales, August 30th, 1850.

W. C. WENTWORTH
J. B. DARVALL
S. A. DONALDSON
COL. SNODGRASS
THE COLONIAL TREASURER
THE AUDITOR GENERAL
THE COLLECTOR OF CUSTOMS
MR. EBDEN
MR· ICELY
MR. MARTIN
MR. JAMES MACARTHUR
MR. WILLIAM MACARTHUR
MR. NICHOLS
C. NICHOLSON, Speaker.

Handbill distributed by Wentworth's opponents in 1850

landowners. In twenty-five years his goal had never changed, but his manner of approaching it certainly had. The year before *Hashemy* he was returned at the head of the poll; in 1851, with Sydney returning three members instead of two, he came in third.

In a speech from the hustings he taunted the mob that shouted him down: 'You may cause it to be written on my tomb *"Here lies the rejected of Sydney"*. But I will venture to prophesy that posterity will add—"who gave to those who deserted him Liberty of the Press, Trial by Jury and the right of electing their own representatives." '

But first or third, he had his seat in the Council, and year after year he struggled on, chairing the Select Committee which was the last milestone on the long journey. Even his opponents admitted that he was the outstanding man of his time. The historian Rusden called him 'the lion of his party . . . A massive form, slouching gait and cast in eye attracted attention if not admiration. His blood is hot, his temper gunpowder, a spark will cause it to explode. But he played the game fairly, was the greatest man in the House, and its greatest orator.'

CHAPTER XV

'GOLD!'

THE events of 1851 made this one of the most important years in the history of Australia.

Up till then, the whole of the settled country had been governed by the British Parliament at Westminster through the Governor of New South Wales. Documents containing decisions were brought across 12,000 miles of stormy seas by sailing ships; after perusal by His Excellency, orders were carried to outlying points of the colony. As the speed of inland communication was no faster than a man on horseback, it often happened that conditions had considerably changed before such orders arrived at their destination.

As sub-colonies formed, each with its own interests and problems, members of these new settlements began to agitate for the right to settle their own affairs. After long argument, and largely owing to the campaigning of Wentworth, the Australian Colonies Government Act was passed. Port Phillip was created a separate colony, to be named Victoria after the Queen, with its own Legislative Council, and similar Councils were set up in Tasmania (formerly Van Diemen's Land), South Australia, and Western Australia.

The new colony of Victoria could be called an infant prodigy, for scarcely was it christened before its name

The wooden convict ship *Success*, one of the first to transport prisoners to Botany Bay

Sydney today

Centre right: Circular Quay with a large liner berthed at the international passenger terminal

was shouted all over the civilised world, linked with another word . . . GOLD!

Way back in 1839, a scientifically minded Polish nobleman, Count Strzelecki, had observed gold particles in the Gippsland region; Governor Gipps, who had already been shown a sample of gold found in New South Wales, asked him as a favour to say nothing about it, fearing lest the news should start unrest and set convicts breaking out to go prospecting. Another geologist, the Reverend W. B. Clarke, had the same experience. 'Put it away, Mr. Clarke,' the Governor urged him, 'or we shall all have our throats cut!' A similar apprehension had long ago caused Governor Macquarie to fear the opening up of the country beyond the Blue Mountains.

In 1849, news blazed round the world of the great gold strike in California. Among the miners who rushed to make fortunes ('Forty-niners' they were called) was one Edward Hargreaves, who went to America from his sheep station on the Bathurst Plains. He did not strike gold in Sacramento, but the appearance of the rocks there reminded him of a winding creek near his home in New South Wales. If gold lay in one, why not in the other? Playing his hunch, he went back to Sydney to try his luck.

Crossing the Blue Mountains on horseback, he spent the night of February 11th, 1851, at a little inn. Shortly after dawn, Hargreaves sallied forth through the forest, carrying a spade, a trowel, and a tin dish. In the cool morning, the tang of the gum-trees told him he was indeed back home, and soon he arrived at the almost dry course of a mountain stream which in rainy seasons dropped into Summerhill Creek.

197

G

In California he had learned the gold-panning drill. Placing a little soil in his tin dish, he washed away the sand and earth—and lo and behold, in the bottom of the plate lay a few specks of gold!

After careful inspection of the neighbouring valleys, Hargreaves wrote to the Colonial Secretary saying that if the Government would give him £500 he would point out localities where gold could be found in abundance. The Secretary wrote back in guarded terms: 'Show us first; cash—perhaps—later'; and a Mr. Stutchbury, the Colonial Geologist, was sent to Summerhill Creek. On May 13th, after discovering a nugget worth £30, Stutchbury gave his opinion that the district was indeed rich in gold.

Five days later, the Summerhill Valley contained about four hundred men stooping over the little creek; within a week, a thousand people were panning for gold in the once lonely gulley.

In alarm the Lands Commissioner wrote to Sydney: 'Some stringent measures should be taken to prevent the labouring classes from leaving their work!' But it was too late. Shepherds abandoned their flocks, merchants closed their stores. Some sold everything they possessed, hurrying off with the idea that gold was lying about waiting to be shovelled into bags. When they saw the toil involved for possibly only an ounce or two of the precious dust, many started for home again, and there was a battling counter-current of disappointed gold seekers passing those starting out hopefully. Needing a scapegoat, they blamed Hargreaves for misleading them, and for a time he feared for his life. However, he received not only his £500, but later on £12,381, in the form of grants by the Victoria and New South Wales governments, and ended up by being presented to Queen Victoria.

The fears of Governor Gipps were well justified. After an aboriginal shepherd discovered a solid lump of gold weighing nearly a hundredweight and worth about £4,000, the stream of hopefuls on the Bathurst Road became a torrent. The Government might as well have tried to stop the tide from coming in. Making the best of it, they appointed a special magistrate, and a police guard to escort the gold back to Sydney. As the land being worked was Crown property, the order went out that diggers must take out licences at the rate of thirty shillings a month.

Down in Victoria, where the settlers had been having a lean time and making little progress for several years, many men began packing up to set off for the goldfields to the north. To stop the leak, Melbourne's leading citizens formed a Gold Discovery Committee, offering £200 to the first who could find a worthwhile goldfield within two hundred miles of the capital. On July 1st, 1851, a miner named Esmond who, like Hargreaves, had learned his lesson in California, found the quartz at Clunes richly veined with gold; he won the prize, but almost on the same day six men found gold only a few miles up the Yarra River on which Melbourne stands.

By now Victoria was alive with diggers. The biggest discovery was made by a man named Cavenagh. Entering an abandoned claim, he dug deeper and came upon some large deposits; he had reached what in past ages had been the bed of a creek, where in every hollow the water had deposited gold brought down from the mountains. Some pockets were worth thousands of pounds.

'Ballarat! Go to Ballarat!' the word went round. Before a month was past, Ballarat was considered the richest gold field in the world. By October, ten thousand men were at work. Acre after acre was covered by circular heaps of red and yellow sand, each with its shaft in the middle in which men were toiling to excavate the soil and pass it to their companions above; these hurried with it to the banks of the creek, where hundreds of 'cradles', rocked by brawny arms, washed gold out of the sand. Other places in the Buninyong Ranges were almost as rich, but even richer were the new discoveries at Bendigo Creek.

On September 17th, a newspaper wrote:

Two bullock carts were being loaded for the diggings with not less than 120 people about them; there were 5 or 6 cradles, wheelbarrows, beds, boxes, frying pans, ovens, pint pots, buckets, guns, sieves, picks, crowbars, spades etc. etc. Geelong is stark, staring gold mad. The custom house hands are off to the diggings, seamen are deserting their vessels, tradesmen and apprentices are gone, their masters following them. Contractors have bolted . . . the doctors and the laymen follow.

Port Phillip was full of ships unable to sail because officers and crew alike had taken the road to the golden land.

Once at the diggings, all men looked alike, dirty and bearded, with slouch hat, ragged shirt and moleskin trousers. Their tents or lean-to huts slumped beside their 'claim', with a piece of bark, nailed on four posts, for a table. Food was a chop or steak straight from the pan, placed on a roll of dough baked in the ashes, called a damper.

From all parts of the world gold seekers flooded in. During 1852, a hundred thousand men of all nations landed in Melbourne, in the following year another 92,000, and by 1856 Victoria had 400,000 inhabitants. Some fantastic finds were made. A Ballarat digger took gold worth £1,800 from a hole in one day. Scott's *Short History of Australia* tells how a party of eight took £12,800 from a claim, and sold it to another party of ten, who dug £10,000 between Saturday and Monday; they in turn sold the working rights for one week to a party of twelve who scooped out £14,400, after which the ten proprietors resumed possession, made £9,000 in the next week and sold out to a party who won £5,000 within the following fortnight. The 'Welcome Nugget' weighed 2,217 ounces and sold for £10,500; the 'Welcome Stranger' was even larger.

The mining camps were scenes of wild drinking, violent fights, and gambling. A shanty town of dance halls and dens sprang up where men who had become rich in the morning could be made beggars again overnight, for the crooks found it easier to get gold from the miners' pockets than from the ground.

Into this mixed assembly poured thousands of Chinese, who came to make quick fortunes and return home. They lived in their own communities, labouring hard and quietly, much to the annoyance of the hard-bitten diggers who made several attacks on them. These clashes caused restrictions to be made on Chinese immigration, and sowed the seed of the 'White Australia' policy, which remains a cause of resentment in Asia to this day.

These were not the only developments which created trouble at the diggings. The licence system was bitterly resented, as the right to dig cost the same for a miner who took thousands of pounds from the ground and the great majority who found little or nothing. The police were in the habit of going 'digger hunting', stopping any man they met and demanding his licence, failure to produce which document could mean being chained to a log for hours or even days. The great mass of miners had no wish for trouble. Twice they sent petitions to Governor Latrobe of Victoria, but without avail. However, in August, 1853, the agitation was becoming so violent that Latrobe hastily reduced the fee from thirty to twenty shillings a month.

Many of those who had flocked to Australia from Europe were revolutionaries; from Ireland came the victims of the potato famine of the 'hungry forties', bearing with them a deep hatred of any authority they deemed to be English. Such an assemblage was happy to foment the grievances of thousands of disappointed miners; the spirit of mob violence spread rapidly over the goldfields, and Latrobe sent out a call for help to the other colonies. Soldiers of the regiment stationed at Hobart were sent up to Melbourne.

At this stage, Governor Latrobe retired from office and was succeeded by Sir Charles Hotham, who took no action, while discontent mounted in the very dry weather that made the creeks too low for panning, though the licence had to be paid. The large body of soldiers encamped near by was bitterly resented, and the whole of Ballarat approached explosion point.

The revolt—when it came—was touched off by a trifling incident. Very late one night in 1854, a digger named Scobie hammered on the door of a disreputable hotel. The owner, an ex-convict named Bentley, rushed out, there was a fight, and in the dark Scobie's head was split open. The acquittal of Bentley by a magistrate who was said to be his business partner led to a riot, with thousands of miners demanding the blood of Bentley to avenge their comrade. Skulls were broken, stones thrown, and Bentley's hotel went up in flames.

Sir Charles Hotham tried to calm down the diggers. Bentley was re-arrested and sentenced to hard labour on the roads, but the men were now in a truculent mood. At a huge protest meeting, the 'Ballarat Reform League' was founded to deal with four grievances: the licence fee, the lack of political rights, difficulties regarding ownership of land, and the Chinese competition. The programme resembled the demands of the English Chartists, adapted to the conditions of the Australian goldfields.

The quarrel had now gone far beyond verbal argument. The troops looked on the diggers as a rebel gang, and in an incident over some waggons the soldiers made a charge, cutting down many people with swords. Enraged, the miners set up a flagstaff, bearing a banner made by their women—of blue silk, with the silver stars of the 'Southern Cross'—under which their elected leaders, the Irishman Peter Lalor and a German named Vern, knelt and solemnly swore to fight to the death. While the military camp was being fortified with loads of firewood and trusses of hay, the miners drilled on the Ballarat slopes with muskets, pistols and spikes stuck on the end of poles, knowing that up from Melbourne were marching eight hundred trained soldiers, marines from men-o'-war in the harbour, and nearly all the police of the colony to put down the newly proclaimed 'Republic of Victoria'.

Against this formidable army, Lalor organised his amateur soldiers to build an entrenchment called the Eureka Stockade (after the claim on which it was erected). Aided by their women, who passionately incited their menfolk to rebellion, they enclosed an acre of ground within a high slab fence, with the 'Southern Cross' floating bravely at the masthead. Both the weather and the emotional temperature were very hot. Knowing full well that the army against them was on the march, the rebels did not expect an attack from the soldiers garrisoned near the camp, and in the evening most of the five hundred defenders left the stockade to take their evening meal and go to bed.

Wise to the situation, Captain Thompson, the garrison commander, decided to put an end to the whole nonsense without more ado, and at dawn on Sunday, December 2nd, 1854, he attacked with 270 of his men.

The battle lasted only a quarter of an hour. Six soldiers were killed, but the casualties among the 'Republicans' were thirty-four, including Lalor, who had a musket ball in the shoulder. Many were taken prisoner.

The Eureka Stockade incident had an importance far beyond a mere skirmish at a mining camp. Everywhere people's sympathies were with the miners. In Melbourne a meeting of five thousand people carried a motion in their favour. Despite a reward offered of £500 for Lalor, he was never taken. When thirteen of the prisoners were brought up for trial, crowds stood cheering outside the building as each was acquitted, and as a consequence the monthly licence fee was abolished in favour of a payment of £1 a year for 'Miner's Rights'.

Eureka Stockade ranked with Peterloo as a rallying cry in the fight for freedom, and it has been said that Australian democracy was born that day at Ballarat.

Growth of Australia's colonisation

CHAPTER XVI

A NEW BEGINNING

THE first wild gold rush died down. The individual digger
with his little tin dish vanished. Though gold continued
to be found in many parts of Australia, the mines
began to be operated by Big Business. Yet the revolt at
Eureka had far-reaching results: for the first time, the
common people of Australia had set themselves up against
authority, and having tasted freedom, they decided never
to allow themselves to be kicked around again.

But hard times were in store, for there were no more
easy fortunes to be picked out of the ground. Most of
those who had struck it rich had squandered their wealth,
lighting cigars with £10 notes and pelting stage perfor-
mers with gold nuggets in the theatres of Melbourne and
Bendigo. Soon the pickpockets were out of work and the
hotel-keepers without customers, as disheartened ex-
miners roamed the country, looking for casual employ-
ment. Bushrangers became so common that they made
fools of the police.

From Sydney, dour Governor Gipps had gone home to
die in 1846, and it was genial Sir Charles Fitzroy who
had presided over the years of the gold rush and the end
of transportation. His equable temper and charming manners delighted Sydney society. Pictures in old illustrated
papers of balls and receptions resemble those of London

at the time, with dashing whiskered officers escorting crinolined ladies of great elegance. Heartily disliking anything unpleasant, Sir Charles left his Colonial Secretary to cope with such trouble-makers as William Wentworth, the upstart demagogue Henry Parkes, and the poet and political agitator, the Reverend Dr. John Dunmore Lang.

No picture of mid-century Sydney would be complete without mention of this turbulent parson, who thundred denunciations of the colony's morals over more than half a century. In the high days of the newspaper war, his *Colonist* lashed out against squatters, governors, and anyone else who had the temerity to differ from his stern line. Though his main interest was the importation of immigrants and the saving of their souls, he was in such continual conflict with authority that at various times he was deposed from the Ministry, sent to prison for libel, and fined £100—which sum was subscribed by his supporters at a shilling per head. Later, he sat for many years in Parliament, representing different constituencies. It was Lang who, with Henry Parkes, led the chorus of ridicule which killed Wentworth's plan for an Australian House of Lords.

Under Wentworth's chairmanship, the Committee which was at last detailed to draw up the Constitution had produced a Bill to give New South Wales a parliament modelled on that of Westminster, for which he had always cherished the greatest admiration. His own pet scheme was an Upper House composed of twenty members, with a new Colonial Peerage created for merit.

The protest against this was Parkes' first public political speech. In language as scarifying as that with which Wentworth himself was wont to flay his opponents, he mocked the idea of a 'mushroom Brummagem aristocracy'. ('Brummagem', a garbled version of 'Birmingham', had become a term for cheap imitation jewellery.) To the poor immigrants and ex-convicts, and especially the Irish, the English upper classes stood for everything they hated most, and to a storm of derision, with sardonic quips about 'Lord Kangaroo' and 'the Duke of Bunyip', the prospective Australian peerage died the death, though the rest of the Bill went through. Shortly afterwards, Wentworth resigned his seat and sailed for England to support the passage through the British Parliament of the Bill which was to be the culmination of his life's work. He was now sixty-three years old. Though his popularity had ebbed away he was still, as his great rival Parkes admitted, 'without doubt the ablest man in the colony'.

One of the achievements for which Wentworth will always be remembered was the founding of the University of Sydney. In 1849 he moved for a Select Committee to enquire into and report upon the best means of instituting a University for the promotion of literature and science, to be endowed at the public expense. As Chairman of that Committee, his Report observed: 'While the Pilgrim Fathers founded a University twenty years after their settlement in America, it is still necessary to send Australian children away from their parents half round the world to get a University education.'

In October, 1850, a Bill authorising the University became law, and the following year Wentworth presided at the first meeting of the Senate, one more reason for deeming 1851 as one of the most important years in Australia's history. In the Great Hall stands a fine statue of the founder by the Italian sculptor Tenerani, which well conveys Wentworth's dogged determination and powerful personality.

The gold rush had only speeded up the change which would inevitably have been brought about by the march of time. The immigrants, English, Irish, and continental European, had come to a new country to work and make their fortunes as free men. The dream of Arthur Phillip in 1788 had been of a country of small farmers, and this was also the official policy which successive Governors had vainly struggled to carry out against the opposition and graft of a gang of individual fortune-builders. Conditions in Australia—her climate and vast distances —could not have been more different from those in England, on which the plan had been modelled. But an idea is hard to kill, and the immigrants had to find out from hard experience that at that time (before refrigeration and quick transport had come into being) Australia was a land more suitable for large sheep-stations than for small mixed farms.

In the days following the gold rush the Australian Legend was born: the ex-digger, lean, bronzed, and independent, who strode over the bushtracks humping his bluey (blanket-roll)—or, as the saying went, 'waltzing his matilda'; he has, through the song by 'Banjo' Patterson, become the symbol of Australia all over the world. From the mutual loyalty of the diggers and 'swaggies', or itinerant labourers, came the quality of 'mateship', which is one of the most cherished characteristics of the Australian tradition.

But not everyone wanted to become a sheep-shearer

and jackeroo, or farmhand. Men had brought out their families, and in the bush notices began to appear:

HOMES FOR THE PEOPLE
Two million acres for selection
on small deposit.

The 'selectors' built their little homes, sowed wheat, and made hay. And the squatters, accustomed to possession of all they could see to the horizon and beyond, were consumed with rage against the 'vermin' who were creeping over 'their' land.

A Government Bill had been drafted to help poor settlers acquire farms on the principle of 'selection before survey'. The idea sounded fine: anyone could enter upon any Crown land, even if it was already leased to squatters, select a few acres, and build his house. Naturally, such a man would choose a plot near a river or waterhole; so would the next selector who came along, and consequently the squatter's flocks would before long find themselves shut off from getting to the water at all.

But that was a game which both sides could play, and the most efficacious method of destroying the upstart farmers was 'peacocking'. Squatters as well as selectors could buy up land, and they knew better than any newcomers the position of the best creeks and waterholes. So the would-be smallholder would often find that the hundred acres in which he had invested all his savings were separated from the stream or river by a strip of land to which he was denied access.

Many of the men and women who bought and farmed land in the mid-nineteenth century went through terrible hardships from droughts, floods, bushrangers and loneliness, and it is they whom many people mean when speaking of the pioneers.

But resolute and brave as the settlers were, it is the explorers of the inland who call forth our greatest wonder and admiration in their attempts—often costing their lives—to 'go before and prepare the way'.

In the earlier days, the explorations of Hume, Sturt, and Mitchell, though arduous enough, had been along river courses in climate that was not too oppressive. By 1845, all that part of Australia which, on a map, would be to the south and east of a line drawn from Brisbane to Adelaide, was fully surveyed. But that still left about seven-eighths of the continent to be explored, and from then on, a constant succession of intrepid men entered the vast central territory to encounter, in addition to hostile aborigines, the perils of hunger, thirst, and sunstroke in that arid desert.

The stories of their exploits have filled many books. Some of their names have come down in Australian history, many more have been forgotten. High on the golden roll of fame are Charles Sturt, the early conqueror of the rivers, who set out again fourteen years later to solve the riddle of the Centre, suffering frightful hardships which ended in total blindness; E. J. Eyre, who tramped all round the Australian Bight from Adelaide to Albany; Kennedy and Gregory; John McDougall Stuart, first man to reach the Centre, who crossed the Continent from South to North; Burke and Wills, who reached the Gulf of Carpentaria from Adelaide and perished on the return journey; and Ludwig Leichhardt, the surly and arrogant German botanist who penetrated three times deep into north-west Queensland before disappearing without trace.

An emigrant ship: from the *Illustrated London News*, 1844

(Patrick White's famous novel, *Voss*, is based on this extraordinary character.)

After the opening up of the Centre came the exploration of the west, and it was not until the turn of the century that the blank spots were finally filled in.

Though the Australian tradition was developed in the bush, many of the new generation were city-born and bred. New towns were springing up, new industries starting. The shape of Australia's future was foreshadowed in the long experimentation of Thomas Mort, a sheep dealer who formed the Sydney Ice Company, the first of its kind in the world, and the engineer Edward

Nicholle, inventor of a method of freezing several tons of meat at a time.

In 1875, a large freezing works was opened at Darling Harbour. At a great banquet the company sat down to eat meat, fish, game, and fruit, all of which had been kept under refrigeration for months. The elaborate dinner over, Mort rose to speak, and his words prophesied a future which today seems commonplace but then sounded like the wildest dream:

> The time is not far distant when the various portions of the earth will give forth their products for the use of each, when the over-abundance of one country will make up for the deficiencies of the other. Climate, seasons, plenty, scarcity and distance will shake hands, and of the mingling will come enough for all. There shall be no more waste.

Two years before Mort's speech heralded the dawn

of prosperity for the graziers and farmers of Australia, the body of William Charles Wentworth, after a state funeral, was buried in a special vault on his estate at Vaucluse, now a national monument. Since his departure to England to see the Australian Constitution Bill, crown of his life's work, through the British Parliament, he had returned to his native land only for a brief period. With his wife and family he made his last home at Wimborne in Dorset, where he lived until his death at the age of eighty-two in 1872. Whatever his faults, his right to the title of Father of the Australian Constitution cannot be disputed. Perhaps his own words are his best epitaph: 'I can truly say that the love of my country has been the master passion of my life.'

As the settled areas of Australia achieved the status of self-governing colonies, the proposal to form them into a Federation gradually passed from discussion to accomplished fact. The outstanding personality in this struggle was Sir Henry Parkes, the picturesque and commanding figure, who had risen from threadbare poverty to serve five terms as Prime Minister before retiring to devote his whole energies to the fight for Federation. With his flowing beard and great leonine head of white hair he was an arresting presence in any gathering, and at last in 1899 he was the means of bringing together the first Australian Federal Convention, which represented the best political brains available at that time.

Parkes had been dead five years when Queen Victoria proclaimed the Commonwealth of Australia, which officially came into being on January 1st, 1901; on May 9th of that year her grandson George, Duke of Cornwall and

York, one day to be crowned King George V, formally opened the first Federal Parliament. Then, in 1931, by the Statute of Westminster, Australia became a Sovereign State.

As a Dominion, Australia sent troops to help the mother country in the first World War, and it was at Gallipoli in 1915 that the nation is said to have 'found its soul'. Since then the heroic but ill-fated landings of the Australian and New Zealand Army Corps have been commemorated on every 25th of April, 'Anzac Day'. It is the one day of the year that touches almost everybody—the old survivors and the relatives of those who did not come back; the marching veterans of World War II, now middle-aged; the new generations and the children. No one who has not been present at an Anzac March can understand the peculiar emotion of the occasion. It does not, as some moderns contend, glorify war. Among the thousands of watchers, some are immigrants to whom Australia has offered refuge from countries torn by war and oppression; often they are ex-enemies, now naturalized and intensely proud of their new country. They are helping in the expansion of prosperity, from the brawny labourers at the great hydro-electric plants which water the parched land to the scientists whose research work helps to bring a fuller life to a country whose population has grown in 175 years from a few hundred persons to nearly eleven million.

On Anzac Day, Australians of all classes feel one people with one history.

BIBLIOGRAPHY

Phillip of Australia, F. Barnard Eldershaw. Melbourne Univ. Press. Out of print.

The Governor's Lady (Mrs. P. G. King), Marnie Bassett. Oxford Univ. Press.

Realms and Islands, Marnie Bassett. Oxford Univ. Press.

John Macarthur, M. H. Ellis. Angus & Robertson.

Lachlan Macquarie; his Life, Adventures and Times, M. H. Ellis. Angus & Robertson.

The Captain General (Macquarie), B. H· Travers. Shakespeare Head.

Macquarie's World, M. Barnard. Melbourne Univ. Press.

The Rum Rebellion, H. V. Evatt. Angus & Robertson.

Sydney's First Four Years, Watkin Tench. (First published in 1890's; recent repub. by Angus & Robertson.).

Sydney Cove, 1788 (original documents), John Cobbett. Hodder & Stoughton.

John Batman, J. Bonwick. Out of print.

Australia's First Patriot, L. Deer and J. Barr. Angus & Robertson, out of print.

The First 100 Years, H. Palmer and McLeod. Longmans, out of print.

Thomas Mitchell, Surveyor General, J. H. L. Cumpston, Oxford University Press.

National Portraits, Vance Palmer. Melbourne University Press.

A Short History of Australia, Ernest Scott. Oxford University Press.

Sydney's Byways of History, Geoffrey Scott. Georgian House, Melbourne.

A Voyage to Terra Australis, Matthew Flinders. Published 1814, out of print.

My Love Must Wait (Biography of Flinders), Ernestine Hill. Angus & Robertson.

The Sydney Scene, Birch and Macmillan. Melbourne Univ. Press.

The Timeless Land; Storm of Time; No Barrier (Factual historical novels, 1788-1813), Eleanor Darke. Collins.

Sara Dane (historical novel), Catherine Gaskin. Collins.

The Australian Encyclopaedia.

My grateful thanks are due to the Trustees of the National Library of Australia, Canberra, and also to the Trustees of the Mitchell Library for allowing me to quote from documents in their possession; also to David S. Macmillan, Archivist of the University of Sydney, for his help and advice.

T. C.

1770 Cook discovers New South Wales

1776 American Declaration of Independence

1788 First Fleet at Sydney Cove (*Arthur Phillip—Governor*)

1789 French Revolution

1790 Second Fleet arrives. W. C. Wentworth born; War renewed with French

1791 *Rights of Man* published

1792 Phillip's governorship ends; United Irishmen formed; Scottish Martyrs transported

1794 Battle 'Glorious 1st of June'

1795 *Captain John Hunter—Governor of NSW*

1797 Macarthur buys merino sheep

1798 Discovery of Bass Strait and Westerport; Flinders and Bass sail round Van Diemen's Land; Nelson in Egypt destroys French Fleet

1799 Pitt outlaws Trade Unions

1800 *Captain P. G. King—Governor of NSW*; Flinders starts *Investigator* voyage; Act of Union with Ireland

1802 Peace of Amiens with French

1803 Flinders circumnavigates Australia; wrecked in *Porpoise*; Settlement tried at Port Phillip; Wentworth to school in England; War with France renewed

1805 Nelson killed at Trafalgar; Battle of Austerlitz makes Napoleon master of Europe

1806 *Captain Bligh—Governor of NSW*

1808 Rum Rebellion: Bligh deposed; Peninsular War in Spain

1809 *Colonel Lachlan Macquarie—Governor of NSW*

1810 Wentworth returns to NSW

1812 Britain at war with America; Castlereagh Foreign Secretary; Luddite riots

1813 Blue Mountains crossed

1815 French defeated at Waterloo; Corn Laws introduced

1816 Bank of New South Wales founded

1816 W. C. Wentworth returns to England

1817 W. C. Wentworth discovers his father's secret

1819 Commissioner Bigge in NSW; Massacre at Peterloo; Wentworth publishes 'Statistical Record of NSW'; Gag Acts passed; Nearly 10,000 convicts transported to NSW

1820 Accession of George IV

1821 *Sir Thomas Brisbane—Governor of NSW*

1823 British Parliament passes Bill for Legislative Council in NSW

1824 W. C. Wentworth back in NSW; publishes *The Australian*; Foundation of Brisbane; Hume and Hovell explore Port Phillip; Tory Reformers at work; Combination Acts repealed; Britain bans slave trade as piracy

1826 *Colonel R. Darling—Governor of NSW*; Sudds and Thompson case

1828 Enlargement of Legislative Council; Sturt discovers Darling River; Settlement at Swan River (W.A.); Publication 'Wakefield Letter from Sydney'; Penal code reformed

1829 Governor Darling recalled; *Sir Richard Bourke—Governor of NSW*

1830 Sturt explores the River Murray; Perth (W.A.) founded; Accession of William IV; Act establishes Trial by Jury, NSW

1832 Reform Bill passed, gives vote to middle classes

1834 Act to establish colony in South Australia; Hentys settle at Portland; 'Tolpuddle Martyrs' transported

1835 John Batman founds Melbourne

1836 Major Mitchell explores Australia 'Felix'; Adelaide founded; Whig reformers at work (education and poor laws)

1837 Melbourne named; Accession of Queen Victoria

1838 *Sir George Gipps—Governor of NSW*

1840 Transportation to Australian mainland discontinued

1843 Legislative Council of 43 members meets

1844 Sturt's journey to the Interior; Leichardt's first expedition

1846 *Sir Charles Fitzroy—Governor of NSW*; Repeal of Corn Laws; Irish potato famine

1850 Western Australia becomes a penal colony; 'Australian Colonies Government Act' passed

1851 Separation of Victoria from NSW; Hargreaves finds gold

1854 Eureka Stockade; Crimean War

1855 *Sir William Denison—last Governor*; Constitution Act —self-government at last (under British Crown)

1872 Death of W. C. Wentworth

1901 Queen Victoria proclaims Commonwealth of Australia

1914 Start of World War I

1915 April 25th: The birth of the Anzac tradition, Gallipoli

1931 Statute of Westminster; Australia becomes self-governing Dominion within the British Commonwealth

INDEX

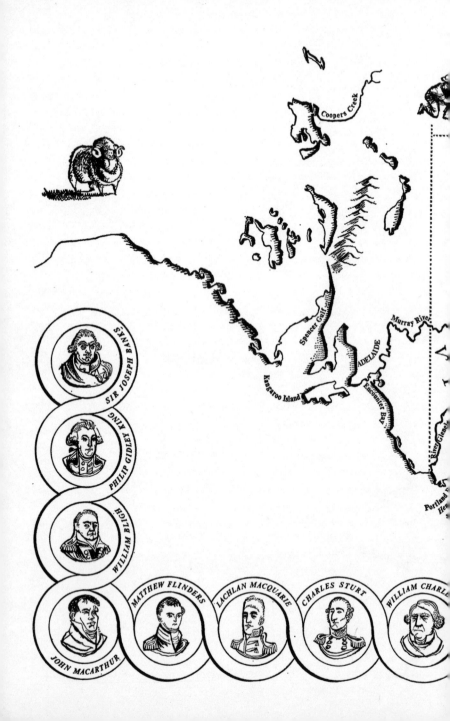

Coopers Creek

Spencer Gulf

Murray River

ADELAIDE

Kangaroo Island

Encounter Bay

River Glenelg

Portland
Head

SIR JOSEPH BANKS

PHILIP GIDLEY KING

WILLIAM BLIGH

JOHN MACARTHUR

MATTHEW FLINDERS

LACHLAN MACQUARIE

CHARLES STURT

WILLIAM CHARLES